Sabbath sense

Sabbath sense

A Spiritual Antidote for the Overworked

by Donna Schaper

Augsburg Books

SABBATH SENSE
A Spiritual Antidote for the Overworked

First Augsburg Books edition © 2005. Copyright © 1997 Donna E. Schaper, International
Copyright secured. All rights reserved. Printed and bound in the United States.

Large-quantity purchases or custom editions of this book are available at a discount
from the publisher. For more information, contact the sales department at Augsburg
Fortress, Publishers, 1-800-328-4648, or write to: Sales Director, Augsburg Fortress
Publishers, P. O. Box 1209, Minneapolis, MN 55440-1209.

ISBN 0-8066-9017-8

Cover design by Hugh Duffy; cover art by Paul Ziegenhagen Slick

Portions of this book have appeared previously in *Stripping Down: The Art of
Spiritual Restoration* by Donna Schaper (copyright © 1991 Innisfree Press, Inc.), and
in *A Book of Common Power: Narratives against the Current* by Donna Schaper (copyright © 1989 Donna Schaper, reprinted by permission of the author).

The paper used in this publication meets the minimum requirements of American
National Standard for Information Sciences—Permanence of Paper for Printed Library
Materials, ANSI Z329.48-1984. ♾ ™

Manufactured in the U.S.A.

09   08   07   06   2   3   4   5   6   7   8   9   10

To my hard-working mother, Eleanor,
who never forgot how to play.

Contents

INTRODUCTION   13

chapter one
SABBATH, THE NEW PLAY ETHIC   19
Dethroning the idol of work.

chapter two
GREAT SABBATHS I HAVE KNOWN   29
Coming home to sabbath.

chapter three
FOR LOVE OR MONEY?   39
Restoring the merry.

chapter four
THE MONDAY CONNECTION   53
Playing at work.

chapter five
SLOWING DOWN   63
Putting margins on the pages of our days.

chapter six
THE UNCONSUMABLE SABBATH   73
Embracing spiritual leisure.

chapter seven
THE SUMMER GARDEN   81
Creating spirit space.

chapter eight
THE WINTER GARDEN   89
Creating sabbath respite.

chapter nine
CLUTTER-FREE LIVING   99
Making room for sabbath.

chapter ten
SPIRITUAL FITNESS   109
Allowing for the unfinished.

chapter eleven
SABBATH RITUALS   115
Taking back our time.

"Find peace
and you will amaze your friends
and confound your enemies."
— Sappho

*I*ntroduction

The idea for this book came to me when I realized that my husband and I and our three children seem to have a lot more fun than other people. We believe that life is more than work! So we have a good time with each other. And the big reason is our sense of Sabbath.

I am a female Christian minister married to a Jewish man, and we have made an interfaith family, celebrating Sabbath on Friday nights with Hebrew prayers and the lighting of the candles, and celebrating the Christian Sabbath on Sundays whenever I don't have to work at my church jobs. We also celebrate Sabbath, moment to moment, by intentionally breaking from work in various ways to honor Spirit.

For generations, "Sabbath" meant Sunday or Saturday to most people: a day when stores closed, churches opened, and families came together to rest and renew their relationship with God. Although the reality of Sabbath as a day of rest has been lost in our busy society, the *sense* of Sabbath, as spiritual leisure, is still very much needed in our time-starved world.

Sabbath Sense is a book for people who think they do not have enough time. It is an ecumenical "how to" that operates on the soul level, a book that invites you to pack your spiritual baggage and move to the neighborhood called Enough — enough time, enough rest, enough play.

There are no "shoulds" in *Sabbath Sense*. This book *can* be read playfully. As Emma Goldman said, "I don't want to be part of any revolution to which I cannot dance." So don't read this book; dance it. Let it become a part of your life and daily rhythms. Sabbath is a rhythm, a tuning into the heart beat and world beat that is slow and beautiful, not fast and frantic. Don't make this book into work. If this book *works* for you, it will be a failure. If this book *plays* for you, it will be its own success.

Sabbath Sense is an antidote to our work-driven culture, an antidote to the anxieties felt in two-career families. As a parish pastor for over twenty years, I have had a front-row seat on life and the near-desperation we have for "time off" from anxiety. With three children, a full-time job, and a nineteen-room house with extensive gardens, I think of myself as a modern, urban, van-driving, quick-chicken-recipe monk. I like my life, I choose it, but I know what people are going through when it comes to time pressure.

Sabbath Sense offers a way to take back our time and take care of our souls — one moment at a time. The focus is on spiritual pauses, not organized-religion-designated days. The sense of Sabbath lies in the moment, any moment that actively includes the presence of God or Spirit. Such moments can include walking, gardening, homemaking, writing — any activity that steals time back from the chaos of a hectic world. Sharing grace at meals, loving the dishes we are wiping, praying with children, meditating, or climbing a weekly mountain — each are rituals that have the potential of unifying our fragmented days and time.

The fragmentation of our minutes and hours is largely why we don't feel we have enough time. When time is broken up into little parts, rather than gathered together into larger ones, it feels too heavy. It loses its shape and its levity. When we ritualize the chaos of modern life, it creates an opening for Sabbath. Rituals keep time from becoming all of the same anxious pace and piece. Rituals separate duty and desire. They allow for leisure, so well-defined long ago as that which we *choose* rather than that which we *must* do. Rituals can even include such unexpected things as keeping house. Traditional women were not wrong in hanging their wash out every Monday. They were onto something the two-career family has lost — ritualizing time so that it can become expansive.

When people today say "my house is a mess," they are usually not kidding. Women suffer particularly around this "failure"to keep their homes "up." Yet even something as simple as a decluttered house can bring a sense of Sabbath. Interior decoration can have a spiritual tilt. Mantels and rocking chairs become places to encounter Spirit. Floral displays in summer can slow time down. Rock gardens in winter can be places of genuine repose. Sabbath moments may be found, informally, in any number of activities, each done in a nearly Benedictine way that honors setting the table as much as any mass. Each path to Sabbath prizes solitude and gives permission to the Inner Hermit in every person. Each takes a few minutes out of full days to bow or nod in a spiritual direction.

This book is about how Sabbath turns not enough time into abundant time. Sabbath invites limited time to become expansive time. Sabbath makes spacious what is cramped. It makes large out of small, generous out of stingy, simple of complex. Sabbath is time that actively includes the presence of Spirit.

Sabbath Sense begins in how to slow down, continues through how to creep, ends with how to stay calm. The method is Sabbath; the purpose is spiritual leisure. I offer *Sabbath Sense* to help you turn not-enough time into enough time, to make a spiritual choice to have time for your own purposes.

Sabbath Sense

chapter one

Sabbath, the new play ethic

Dethroning the idol of work.

Sabbath is a state of mind, not a day of the week.

Sabbath used to mean a specific day: Sunday for Christians, Saturday for Jews. It was the day taken off from work for religion and for rest.

It was not a day for watching television, with its dramatic replacement of our story with someone else's story. It was not a day for hiking, with its grand viewpoints and body-changing, feel-good potential. Nor was it time to do errands or catch up on desk stress or pay bills or run errands. Sabbath was designated specifically for "religious" rest.

Work stopped. Rest started. Sabbath organized society's time into a rotation of weekdays and weekends. Stores closed; churches and synagogues opened. Religious institutions had their dedicated time. Youth had youth groups; families had "Sunday dinners."

But our culture has not taken Sabbath of this kind for a long time. Blue laws that kept stores closed on Christian Sabbaths are long gone. Many people work on weekends. Kids play soccer. Errands and household chores and social obligations fill up the calendar. If the desk is going to get unstressed, Sabbath is about the only time we have to do it. Because of these enormous changes in the way our week is structured — and our work and play are structured — the meaning of Sabbath has all but disappeared. Time for spiritual rest is a luxury.

In our middle-class society today, fewer and fewer people organize their lives by religious institutions that conveniently separates time into "work" and "rest" slots. We work most of the time. We imagine little time off. We think we have obligations most of the time. We imagine little time for deeper emotions, like joy or weeping. A good hymn sing and memory of Grandma's funeral seems almost quaint. All time seems the same. It is as homogenized as the milk and the neighborhood. Time is the river in which we rush from one place to another. Time is money, or so we say in the world without Sabbath.

Sabbath comes from the word "to separate," as in one of its roots, "sabbatical," where scholars still separate "teaching time" from "study time."

Sabbath is the separation of time into different parts. Sabbath is neither rest nor labor but the separation of the two. Sabbath is the pause between them.

Time without Sabbath, without separation, is time that is homogenized by anxiety. The simple name of the anxiety is the Protestant work ethic — the belief that hard work produces happiness. The majority of us subscribe to its articles of faith. Are its time and usefulness over? Even if we are ready to declare the work ethic obsolete, many of us still carry it around like an old record or cartridge tape. We don't know whether to throw it out or hang on to it. Maybe we'll need it someday . . .

The number of people who still believe in work is high, but the connection between work and happiness is low. The work ethic has turned hollow: it has become a "should." Work *should* produce happiness. But most of us know that work in this society does not produce happiness. The work ethic drives us, but it does not get us "there."

Consider how many people you know who want to retire early. Ask teachers to report on satisfaction in their work. Or farmers. Or executives. Or machinists. Or housewives. Or doctors. Or interrogate those in my own profession, the ministry, which has gone from being a "high-status, low-stress job" to being a "low-status, high-stress job," as Loren Mead, retired executive director of the Alban Institute, puts it so well. If you can find a group of workers who work hard because working hard brings them happiness, report to me right away.

The majority of us are working harder now than we did twenty years ago. But we are not finding more happiness. Just the opposite is true. It does not take long to see the basic problem: The connection between work and happiness is broken.

The work ethic does not work — but that does not mean that people in this society have stopped believing in it. Because of the disconnection between work and happiness — and people's awareness of the disconnection — we face an ethical crisis, if not an emergency. We are living by a belief that we do not really believe. That which we think will save us does not save us. Work does not make us happy. But we have constructed our families and our economic culture around the bedrock belief in this broken connection.

In this death-of-the-work-ethic, we face both a spiritual and a material crisis. We do something every day that is supposed to be good but does not feel good. We are daily disappointed. We are disappointed both materially and spiritually, both in our everyday experience and in our own confidence level. Why is work so stressful when everyone says it should be so good?

In the last few decades, working hard as a mode of exchange is a value that has exceeded its boundaries. It has become in charge of parts of life where it has no business being in charge. There are some parts of life that are still sacred: They are the parts that have no price tag. We get to have them even if we are not rich or do not work hard. They are what we used to call grace.

Economic transactions have taken over more and more of the places where grace might still prevail. Universities have become more dependent on corporate contributions. Mention college and the average parent thinks cost. The art world has become more than ever a place to buy and sell. Good plays cannot just be good plays; they have to "make it" on Broadway. Welfare is becoming workfare. Getting sick is more about the fear of how to pay for the illness than it is about getting over the illness.

While taking very seriously the crisis of the American economy — where the rich get richer and the poor get poorer — I do not think that saving it is the highest value. Cost containment or bottom lines is not a decent driving force for anything, especially a life. Human *being* is the higher value. And our human *doing* has to be connected.

We face an interpretive emergency. When did the goodness of work stop and the drudgery start? Was the work ethic ever a good thing around which to build a society? Did work stop producing happiness — and did that result in the spiritual crisis? Or did work's inability to produce happiness produce the spiritual crisis? In actuality, I think both cause and effect tangle us in a knot. Work ceased to be meaningful, thus causing a spiritual crisis. Our spiritual crisis then allowed work to become meaningless. It is a tangled web in which spiritual failure joined material greed, which then created more spiritual failure — which then systematized into a political/economic/spiritual knot.

Sabbath is one of the casualties of our hypocritical work ethic. Instead of trying something *different* — as Pogo said long ago in the phrase, "Don't just do something, stand there" — we just work harder! We make work and obligation out of family festivals. We make work and obligation even out of our leisure. I see people rushing to their ski resorts on Friday afternoon so they will not be late. The same people use a cellular phone at their summer campsite. I have these people in me; they are not a "them." We are a "we." I can easily go for weeks at a time, feeling harried and pushed by something I cannot quite explain. It is not God. It is not good. It is certainly not beautiful. It puts a long frown on my face, a high-pitched tone in my voice, and does not do a thing for my heart or liver or lungs.

When we lost Sabbath, we lost the sacredness of time.

And we let it happen to ourselves. No one gave us the virus; we self-inoculated. Ten years ago I never would have thought of calling my answering machine from my summer vacation. Now I cannot imagine *not* calling it. I am not alone.

We are not without hope. The malady is not

necessarily fatal. Rather than being an alarmist about the death of the work ethic, I gladly herald a new play ethic: *Sabbath Sense.* A true play ethic that praises graceful idleness. That recreates nearly lost or forgotten parts of life, like porch-swinging and playing cards, deep repose, Sabbath dinners, and just plain loafing.

Many people are uncomfortable with the very idea of "play." We would rather "*do* something." Sabbath Sense is not opposed to work. It is not anti-work. Rather, it is a way of putting work in its proper place. Sabbath Sense restores our ownership of our own time. Sabbath Sense gives us time for wearing both work boots *and* dancing shoes. Sabbath Sense has a chance of restoring meaning to the work place.

To dethrone the idol of work, it is important to clarify what work actually is. Many of us still find a little too much joy in suffering — especially if it is other people's suffering. "It's good for them," we say. But work, in its broadest sense, is anything we *have* to do; play, anything we *may* do. Sabbath as a new ethic of play separates "must" from "may," duties from desires, obligation from freedom.

Sabbath is the Continental Divide that separates time with its price tags "on" from time with its price tags "off." Both kinds of time have moral legitimacy. But neither has the right to tyrannize the whole of our time. We do not need to be ruled by a life of economically-rewarding work. Nor do we need to be continually at play, with no work to do. Ask someone who has nothing to do, ever again! They have lost some essential capacity, and they will tell you the tyranny of grace without works. The old Yiddish proverb is useful here: *The worst thing to carry is having nothing to carry.*

Sabbath is also the connection between rest and labor. Sometimes we rest at work. Or work at rest. Sabbath is choosing the time in which they are known to be different. Sabbath is a process. It is a way of living. By observing Sabbath, we become persons who both work and rest, and know why, when, and how we do either. We also know the occasions on which we do both, at the same time. Observance of Sabbath and its separation of time into work and play paradoxically unifies our time. It makes it all ours. Sabbath is the spiritual choice to have our time for our own purposes. Sabbath people know our time and how we want to use it. In the same spirit that many women "take back the night," we take back our time.

Since Sabbath is no longer clearly defined by society's or religion's rules, Sabbath is a discipline we have to make and do ourselves. We have to choose participation — either in formal, structured religious institutions, or in personal or communal spiritual practices of our own. And we have to surmount the obstacles that block our regular participation — whether economic or familial. The obstacles also include our own fatigue as we live too many working lives in too short a week. If we do not separate our own time, no one will do it for us.

Sabbath Sense is anything that makes spacious what is cramped. That makes large out of small, generous out of stingy, simple out of complex, choice out of obligation. Sabbath Sense is anything that reconnects the necessities of drudgery to the marvelous uselessness of beauty. Sabbath Sense is acknowledgment of the presence of Spirit in the petty and the profound.

Sabbath Sense may be the chair we sit in when we come home, the coffee we enjoy once we get to work, the clothes we put on for a special occasion. Sabbath may be the breakfast out we have with each of our children before going to work on Friday. It may be simply a moment of memory at "off" times during the day or year. Sabbath may be choosing to remember Grandma every year, not just on the day of her death, or her birth, but by making Grandma's beef stew recipe. Or by wearing the ring she gave us to church or synagogue on a festival day. Or by going out dancing. Sabbath may also be deliberate, organized "goofing off" on the job. It may be hurrying up on some things so we can go slow on others.

Sabbath is time spent remembering what time is for.

——— ———

I think of an African speaker at the podium at a World Council of Churches meeting. The nervous moderator informed the African that he only had three minutes. The African objected with great dignity, "I doubt that I only have three minutes, Mr. Moderator. I am an African and I take my time."

*G*reat sabbaths I have known

chapter two

Coming home to sabbath.

When I was a parish pastor and conducted my own Sunday services, I got a taste of what good Sabbaths are about. They are times to remember the ancient texts and to think about them in a contemporary context. They are a time to sing. They are a time to forget about ourselves. A time to be quiet together. A time for filtered light. A time for lit candles. A time for preludes and postludes, marked beginnings and endings. Sabbath is a time to let go of the past, to receive a blessing, to be reminded that it is possible to go on. Sabbath is a time to learn more about the core of the universe. It is a time to be in sanctuary, safe space, to look out the windows and know we are safe inside.

Sabbath is time out of time. It is time that ends one week and prepares for another. Sabbath keeps time by keeping the beat. It gets us out of one kind of time into another kind of time on behalf of the very time we left. Without Sabbath, the weeks get weird. With Sabbath, we learn to press our stop key and our start key.

Now that I am what is called a "circuit rider" and work as an Area Minister with episcopal responsibility for over one hundred churches, I don't find as much "Sunday" Sabbath in my life. I miss the preparation of the text, the putting together of the bulletin or the order of service, the choosing of a title and focus for the sermon, the actual writing of the sermon, the selecting of the hymns and psalms and lay readers. Without the anticipation, I find Sabbath a bit small. Sabbaths that other people have prepared, once you have prepared your own, are a bit skinny.

My leaving the parish ministry — for very good reasons of a larger ministerial nature — was surely the catalyst for writing this book. I had to learn other ways, beyond Sunday practice, to keep Sabbath.

I have learned to be less "churchy" about Sabbath. I have learned that neither God nor the Sabbath is caged in the church. Most certainly, God is not the end point of my liturgical efforts! We can find God in almost any regular practice. We can even find God in irregular practice.

I think of the times my family has hosted regular potlucks. In Philadelphia, years ago, we used to have regular Sunday dinners and pick up people from whoever was at church that Sunday. I loved cooking for these events; I loved the table conversation. I loved the surprises of who would come and what they would say to each other. One day we had people from Nigeria, Texas, the Philadelphia church, the neighborhood, and some members of my own family. I remember thinking as we said the Sunday prayer, holding hands, that God was at this table. "This," I am sure I heard Her say, "is how I mean for my people to be. Laughing together, eating good food together, relaxing into each other's space."

I remember the Friday night observances of the Jewish Sabbath we held in Amherst for a group of local politicians and "human service" types. (These people are rarely fed; they are almost always doing the feeding.) These "colloquies" as Sabbaths were a time that people who ran shelters and soup kitchens could talk with faculty and politicians from other local institutions. The food was always fabulous (as the Philadelphia potlucks were wont to be), the conversation shy at first and deeper later. These Sabbaths were times of political connection and community building; they were also designed to let our children "overhear" what adults wanted to say to each other. The only ritual was a simple Hebrew prayer and a lighting of the candles.

Our interfaith family keeps Sabbath on Friday nights in a similarly simple way. We have tried to do the whole ritual at table on Friday, and we have failed. For a long time, the children were just too small to keep attention. My husband wanted nineteenth-century children who could sit still right before a meal for fifteen minutes, and he didn't get them. He and I would often get into squabbles over the developmental capacities of seven-year-olds — and so went the long form of Sabbath.

Now that we do a shorter form on Friday nights, things are fairly undramatic but lovely. (We could probably do a longer form now but at some expense to our established simplicity.)

The ritual we use in praying with our children is to invite them to say something for which they are grateful that happened today. We are often surprised! Our son Jacob, at age seven, found a way to tell us that his classmate had been through a great tragedy:

"Yvette is back."

"I didn't know Yvette was gone."

"Her mother died after they chopped her breast off."

Later it was possible to talk to Jacob about Yvette, and the missing breast, and death. Sabbath prayers let the conversation happen.

We also do a nightly ritual, after the invitation about something good, which prays to the One I call the breath God, or the big God, or the God beyond God. It is a childish prayer because it began when the children were three- and four-years old. Now we do it with twelve- and fourteen-year-olds. It has gathered meaning by repetition:

> *"God, be above us,"*
> (we pray as the hands go up all around),
> *"God, be below us,"*
> (our hands go down).
> *"God, be all around us,"*
> (we use both hands to make concentric circles in the air in a lively way),
> *"and, God, be with our friends . . ."*

Then we name anyone who is missing. Each of us, now that we are all so mobile, appreciates being remembered by whoever is there in this way. My daughter, Katie, once asked me once if we remembered her when she was at a friend's. We also have long conversations about who our friends are. Do you have to know somebody to pray for them? I don't think so.

Great Sabbaths I have known — Sunday Sabbath, Friday Sabbath, prayers at meals, conversations at meals, time at table as sacred time — all fit into this basic, simple context. I love praying with the children right after the pizza comes to Room 429 in the motel. I love doing our little table grace in restaurants and watching the kids do (but hide) the hand motions. I love escaping stuffy church services in order to get out into traffic to talk with God.

The Communion ritual for me is also a deeper Sabbath, and I like to worship with the local Episcopalians just to get more frequent holy and ritual "food" in the weekly Eucharist. I like to worship with a black Baptist church down the street to get more frequent praise.

I also like to do *t'ai chi* at dawn on the town common, when I can get to it, as a more physical Sabbath. I was so deeply moved in Beijing by the crowds in motion in the street every day at dawn. The old men "walked" their birds; the old women moved their bodies vigorously. The younger men and women did the same, although with much greater dexterity. They were keeping Sabbath; they were moving their bodies to a God-like rhythm.

I fear I am a post-modern when it comes to the sense of Sabbath. I go every which way to find God. Many channels seem open to me. I wouldn't say that I have a remote clicker in my hand to keep changing channels so much as that I have a lust for Sabbath. I like its interruption of ordinary time with sacred time.

When I was growing up, my family kept Sabbath in the traditional Protestant Lutheran way: Sunday was more social than spiritual. (I think that is where I first learned that God loves people, that the spiritual comes through the social!) In the fifties, we had very little to do on Sunday except for visits back and forth between families. Nobody talked about much except each other. There was always a large dinner somewhere, usually at a grandparent's house. People drank beer. People told secrets. The women talked about the men in the kitchen. The children ran around in circles doing cousin-type things. We fought. We told secrets. We stole things from each other. We played endless hide-and-seek. We played "Mother, May I" for afternoons that seemed more like decades in the front yard. The men occupied chairs and talked sports, or bosses, or cars, or routes to take to Peekskill. People were not rushing; they were *being*. There was no where to go but where they were.

The day started with Sunday School, then the church service at eleven a.m. There was a kind of serious inattention to these things that we did every Sunday, no matter what. I find now that I have absolutely no idea what the pastor ever spoke about, even though I have perfect attendance pins for a dozen years. I do know the words to every hymn by heart, and I love singing them without a book. And I can recite most of the psalms. (Now that we have made the language more inclusive, I miss a lot of beats, but I don't care. I love the memories.)

My parents lived in a more congealed time and a more congealed culture; I live in a less congealed time and a less congealed culture.

My own private rituals for Sabbath are usually quite physical. I pray by giving attention to my body, not my mind, or even my soul. I am closest to my sense of God when I am out of my head. If I really want to hear more deeply the sacred beat of time, I need to get physical. To dance. To do some yoga. To do some *t'ai chi*. To walk.

I use the physical rituals as a discipline for five personal foci. First, I meditate on the word "enough." Secondly, I make a Sabbath effort to play at my work and to work at my play. My third direction is to connect my inner life to my outer life. Fourth, I meditate on the meaning of the Christian creed that promises the resurrection of the body and life everlasting. I consider the paradox of becoming more youthful over time. Fifth, I try to understand the sacrament of marriage as deeply as I can: as a nest and hope for my family and my deepest personal connection to others.

How are these disciplines Sabbaths? They interrupt my ordinary time with sacred purpose. They connect me over time to life purpose. I embody myself in these Sabbaths. I do these things to connect my body to my spirit, to connect ordinary time to sacred time. Church services can be the link to Sabbath, as can candles — or prayers at table or in motel rooms. Or walking or standing on our heads in a yoga posture.

I used to have as life goals different things. I wanted to "enjoy God" and "befriend the poor." I still want to do these things, but over time, I have come to understand more about how to enjoy God and befriend the poor. The cultural key to the friendship with the poor is becoming a culture that has enough for everyone. The personal key is becoming rich enough to care. Not physically rich, although that helps, but spiritually rich enough not to need to forget the suffering of the poor. The key to enjoying God is to remember that God is everywhere, not just inner and not just outer, but in history, and economics, and yoga, and clouds. The key to enjoying God is to know that God is near.

I change these life goals and meditations from time to time. Before the enjoyment and the friendship goals, I had only two goals: to be funny and to be skinny. When I realized I was about to turn fifty, I decided I needed to become a more serious person. On behalf of my grandmother, whose table created a Sabbath space almost any time, anywhere, I added the goal of generosity to my goals of humor and thinness. My grandmother's laughter brought God to any occasion.

The foci of my meditations will change again. The point of the focus is to find sacred time, not that any one focus dare survive all of life's developments and changes.

We each have different ways to find our life purpose and to embody it. We don't have to be "home" in a congealed culture or our own house to know the sense of Sabbath. We don't have to be Missouri Synod Lutherans or Orthodox Jews to keep Sabbath. We don't need an instruction manual. We can make our own way to God. Sabbath's sense brings us home and makes a home wherever we are.

Sabbath Sense

chapter three

For love or money?

Restoring the merry.

Children love carousels. The hurdy-gurdy music. The majestic carved horses, nostrils flared, hooves perpetually poised to gallop. The fanciful circus animals. The heady mix of fantasy and reality. And then the ride, gently swaying, up and down, wooden ponies posed in prance, whirling round and round. The kids laugh and chatter. But when we grow up, the merry-go-round becomes a metaphor not for play but for work we can't escape. "Stop the merry-go-round; I want to get off" becomes our cry.

That is because we have lost a sense of Enough. We have lost a sense of Time. We have lost a sense of Enough Time. Life seems all merry-go-round, without the merry. Too much PAY and not enough PLAY. Restoring Sabbath does not eliminate the merry-go-round, but it does reinsert the merry.

Sabbath restores time by an act of memory. It remembers what life was like when our ride on the merry-go-round was merry! It remembers that Spirit is part of our time and that we are part of Spirit's time.

Returning to a sense of Sabbath requires just the opposite of effort — which is, remarkably, the hard part. We want to *do* something to make things happen, when, in fact, stopping our obsessive doing is just what we need. Returning to a sense of Sabbath is remarkably simple. There are three basic pathways: *personal, political,* and *spiritual.*

———   ———

The *personal* path to reviving Sabbath Sense is learning to be right where we are. Even if where we are is on an assembly line. Or at the kitchen sink. Or in front of a computer monitor. Just being where we are is a radical step in a society such as ours where the cultural instructions are loudly stated: "MOVE ON, MOVE OVER, MOVE UP, MOVE, MOVE, MOVE, MOVE!! From "Go west, young man," to "climb every mountain," this culture has committed itself to insatiable instability. We forget what *enough* means or could mean.

Rabbi Zusya of Hanipol once started to study a volume of the Talmud. A day later, his disciples noticed that he was still dwelling on the first page. They assumed that he must have encountered a difficult passage and was trying to solve it. But when a number of days passed, and he was still immersed in the first page, they were astonished but did not dare to query the master. Finally, one of them gathered courage and asked him why he did not proceed to the next page. Rabbi Zusya answered, "I feel so good here, why should I go elsewhere?"

To revive Sabbath Sense, we have to give ourselves the time to *be*, where we are. To protect our humanity, we have to be committed to paying attention to ourselves and to what happens to us.

In every one of our experiences, there is much more happening than we ever notice. Henry David Thoreau once said he could find the whole world in Concord! Mostly, we don't find the meaning, or the merry, in our experiences because we don't reflect on them. Paying attention to what is happening right where we are — and commenting on it — can be a very exciting way to live. That is mindfulness in action. Even if it is Sunday Sabbath, Friday Sabbath, prayers at meals, conversations at meals, time at table as sacred time. Even if it only means saying aloud, "I felt dead at work today." We don't have to resolve every feeling we can find words for. But we do have to find the words.

41

The capacity to be happy where we are is pretty much lost in the modern world. Most of us like the page we are on quite well. It's just that we are also looking over our shoulder at the next page to something "better." The next obligation invades the current obligation. We could really enjoy our son's soccer match if it weren't for the groceries we should be picking up later. These invasions of "now" by "later" are insidious, a form of mental enslavement. As someone described a woman who was marrying her third husband, "She likes him well enough, but she is already looking over his shoulder for something better." So goes the hunt for a better house, a better car, a better stereo. It is a kind of lust, and it is lethal. When we are no longer insatiably bent on The Next Thing, we are much less likely to be enslaved, and we undercut the possibility of others — or time — owning us.

Spiritually-fit persons understand just how much there is in everything. We don't need the crazy venture for more. We are able to see a lot in a little. Able to be lost in time. Able to *be*. When we can have little victories over of *being* over *doing*, we can find our way to the Sabbath of enough.

———   ———

Another route to restoring the sense of Sabbath is *political*. When the women's movement spoke about

how intensely "the personal is the political," this
paying attention to human being in the social
environment is very much what they meant. Judith
Plaskow, a Jewish feminist theologian, posits that
the political may exist to protect the spiritual, and
I think she is right. Happiness does not always come
from work, but work is the prelude to food on the
table. Politics protects our capacity to get food on
the table so we don't have to overworry about food.

For most of us, the anxiety of an empty table
is too much to sustain alone. That's why we need
each other, for a minimal level of protection for our
humanity. You and I can "be" all we want, but
without collective wind at our back, society can get
rid of us pretty quickly. By paying radical attention
to who we are and where we are, we can reorganize
our political structures not so much from an activist
perspective as from a human perspective.

To accomplish this restoration, we have to
help our society's various institutions — universities, medicine, law, churches, synagogues, journalism — to pay attention to themselves, to their true
selves, to their original purposes of better serving
the public. If you read the mission statements of
most colleges, for example, you find that they, in
fact, do exist to serve others, not to balance their
books. Hospitals exist to heal the sick, not to make
profits. Journalists exist to tell the truth, even if that
does not flatter advertisers. Churches exist to save

souls, not to get souls to pay their bills.

Yet the ends of work are too often ignored; the means of work are overmassaged. The why of what we will do is barely mentioned; the ways we will do things are endlessly discussed. To our misguided political leaders, too often the point is "growth": to maximize questionable means for that spurious end. As if the environment could take any more first-world growth. As if people could work any harder than we already do. As if our present moments could be any more invaded and enslaved by duty than they already are. As if we needed more things to stumble on in our homes. The material clutter of the moment is not even noticed, so furiously are we in pursuit of *more* of it.

There are economic and political alternatives:

- ⟡ What if we guaranteed annual incomes that would allow artists and inventors to flourish? (We have the money but not the will!)

- ⟡ What if we fostered a new kind of journalism, one of many small, local papers, instead of supporting only the three or four big ones?

- ⟡ What if we started a new kind of law and a kind of medicine, preventive in nature, that got so radically to the cause of illness and crime that paradoxically they rendered their professions less urgent, less "useful," less "growth industry" over time?

⋄ What if we removed big baseball's antitrust exemption? That could turn that "work" into regional play very quickly!

⋄ What if we stopped blaming the poor for being poor? When Ann Richards, former governor of Texas, quipped that "middle-class women are immoral for abandoning their children to wage work, and poor women are immoral for not abandoning them," we know just what she meant!

Growth is not mandatory. Work is not *de-facto* moral. Most comfortable Americans could stand to live with a lot fewer things — especially if they could trade for time and a reduction of the stress of work and consuming. In terms of sheer expenditure of energy and human effort, we are already producing more than we can afford to produce. We are working too hard to be able to keep buying that excess.

We need to activate our memories. Early in life we heard that technology and computers would *liberate* us for leisure, not *replace* our leisure. That sustained economic growth would make our economy less idolatrous, less exploitative of the powerless, less an invasion of our actual lives, and more of a goal we could love. We need to remember that sustainable economic growth creates the possibility of play; unlimited growth requires the stick of duty that beats play out of us. Sustainable growth is sensible — it restores Sabbath and Sabbath Sense; unsustainable growth means that we will never have enough time.

Spirit is possible in one of these worlds and squeezed out in the other. Spirit infuses in one, refuses in the other.

These political realities govern our personal lives. More and more of us dream of a time when we could rest and play, a time when we could even get stuck on a page and perhaps linger there. I almost don't know anyone who is *not* overwhelmed. The rich are overwhelmed by the challenge of spending and investing their wealth. The poor are overwhelmed by the obscenity and grinding relentlessness of their poverty. And those of us in the middle are working harder than we ever have before and enjoying it less.

Essentially we are held hostage by the perceived virtue of growth, overzealously sustained by the old work ethic gone sour.

The litany is familiar even to newcomers to our culture: Work hard, get along. Work hard, things go well. The promise is that effort yields happiness. Most of us sing this tune all day long — through clenched teeth. If we have another tune playing, it is only on our private headset.

The insidious victory of the work ethic is that of "means" over "end." As Christopher Fry wrote in *The Lady's Not For Burning*, "I gave you mystery and paradox and what you want is cause and effect." The capacity to enjoy, at times even to imagine, an end, a thing for itself — an unmedicated, undedicated moment — is nearly lost on us. Play has lost the battle to work. The invasion, then enslavement, is first mental and psychological, then material and political.

Play is valuing a thing for itself. Ask any child playing blocks on the floor. Or a mother folding laundry in a home she loves. Or a father building a play-house in the backyard. Or someone working as a person on a computer instead of operating as a machine. Or even an activist plotting a demonstration.

To move from the old work ethic to the new play ethic requires surprisingly little effort. We have to BE more and DO less. We have to linger. We have to go slow. We have to refuse the culture's instructions to go fast. We have to be where we are when we are there. We have to refuse our orders to move along.

Buddhists talk about "Monkey Mind" getting in the way of meditation. Monkey mind, which jumps from subject to subject, interferes with our sense of time. It tears time apart. The play ethic, which rebalances Sabbath's simultaneous appreciation of work and play, puts time back together. As in the words of the marriage ceremony, it lets no one tear asunder, or pull apart, what God has joined together.

Play is a form of building and creating — an art — but it is also subversive. Every time we do something for the sake of doing it, we subvert the old work ethic. Every time we linger, we subvert it. We don't have to do much at all to allow the play ethic to emerge in us. We in fact have to do *less*.

This is the heart of the strategy for restoring Sabbath, personally, politically, and spiritually: BE MORE; DO LESS!!! All of us. Only then can we restore Sabbath. Only then can we move from the hollowness of the work ethic to a fuller play ethic. Only then can we both work and play. Only then can we understand the virtue of both *doing* and *being*.

———   ———

Recovering a sense of Sabbath by a *spiritual* road depends on how we see ultimate reality. We need to disbelieve the bosses and rebelieve our own and our community's best selves. Neither the personal nor the political have a chance if they are not grounded in the spiritual, if we do not believe that we have value without our work. That does not mean that we should not work, but rather that we can unload work from the heavy baggage of carrying our value.

Many of us were taught that work is supposed to be a vocation, something we do for the end of glorifying life and God. Still, most of us work for the sake of our paycheck. We work for bread, and "Bread." For the means of bread. Not for the goal of life to which bread is dedicated. There is a kind of work that could reduce the enslaving power of "Bread." Work that would bow less at the altar of global overgrowth and more at the altar of sufficiency. Less to duty and more to play. Work that is not all play but has *play* as its point.

Politically and spiritually the trick is the same: We have to reinvent leisure, relegitimise life outside the job. The highest ideal of labor known to humanity is work that becomes play. Work that we own and want to do. To accomplish this will take a labor movement that is dedicated to more than labor!

Because so many of us are biblical and spiritual amnesiacs, we only faintly remember the ancient echo that we do not live by bread alone — and then we go right out and live by bread alone. When we live by more than "Bread," we open the space in our lives to live for Spirit. We have the sense of Sabbath.

Our economy desperately needs us to take time off from feeding itself on "Bread." It needs rest as much as we do. All the arguments about Sunday "blue laws" suddenly come home to roost. Why *do* all the stores need to be open on weekends? We know the answer. But look at what has happened to our days. As Rabbi Abraham Heschel has said in his eloquent essay "The Sabbath," "Time loses its beauty when every day is the same." Beauty is the chief victim in the war of production against play.

The ways the work ethic can become a play ethic are highly practical. What is impractical and unsustainable is the current global scale of greed, and most of us know it. We just don't take the spiritual risk of living as though that were true.

We need to redefine supply and demand for a new Sabbath economic. As John Henry Cardinal Newman has said, the real task of the university is "not to supply people to meet an existing demand but to create the sort of people who create a new sort of demand."

An economic program I could sign up for would slowly reduce — or humanize — the so-called American standard of living. So our children could buy their own homes, rather than having a war with our generation over equity. So that the two-career family — which is absolutely not sustainable — could be a thing of the past. So that people had to work only thirty hours a week and had more time for church and synagogue, piano and drama, reading the Torah one slow page at a time. That kind of economic policy — a smaller one, not a larger one — is an economy that acknowledges play and rest, rather than just work and production. That kind of economy will result only from a simultaneous personal, spiritual, and political restructuring. Anything less will be wanting.

That is an economic program that will work — and play — in the future. If we go for more, instead of less, we only hurt ourselves. Terribly. Even as we do every day right now, rushing, rushing from page to page. We structure the injustice more deeply. The goal of NAFTA is more. The goal of globalization is more. Do you really want to be the head of the world's body? Do you really want the rest of the world to be your muscles? Can you bear that injustice-masquerading-as-necessity?

I can't. I also want to be able to live in my own body and not just in my head. To do my own gardening and my own wash and to live connected to bodily things. As I move "up" in my own profession, I find a literal conspiracy to keep me from doing my own housework! I *want* to wash my own dishes and do my own laundry. I *like* the feel of hot soapy water, the look of clean dishes. In these everyday, unglamorous domestic chores I find some Sabbath Sense.

These visions of work dedicated to the Spirit rather than bread — to *being* rather than *doing* — may sound naïve, especially to the person who finds there is a lot of month left at the end of the money. Naïve in a world where women are overchallenged and men are overprotected by large scale economic institutions. But consider how much human effort has been negated due to technological "advances"

— how can we label them *advances* until the social component catches up? — such as voice phone and electronic mail and automatic tellers. To change any of these large scale directions — particularly with the poor around the world getting poorer while others more comfortable get richer — will require a large-scale intervention. An intervention at the highest level. And at the lowest level. What some would call revolution.

Many of us might even sign up for that revolution. But first we'd want to be totally clear about the goal. The goal of sustaining our being, not increasing our being. The goal of play and pleasure over work and duty. The goal of Sabbath. Humans not as capital or as machines or as gods, but humans as humans. Humans, being. Reclaiming the merry in merry-go-round.

chapter four
The monday connection
Playing at work.

Playing at work is more practical than working at work: Playing produces more with less effort. The play ethic is much more plausible than the drudgery and despair of the work ethic: It restores freedom to labor. Many of us could do much more at our jobs if we didn't feel so beholden to them. Duty does not produce. Grace does.

Though the belief that we "should" work is fundamental to most of us, very few people argue that the work ethic still works. They agree that it pushes people in android rather than human directions. The work ethic is spiritually bankrupt. We are desperate for something new, different, and better. Yet most people also think a new play ethic is impractical. They are even embarrassed by it possibilities.

Sabbath time — and play time — is not utopian or idealistic. It is possible. It is pragmatic. It is even the highest practicality. We need to start on a small, human level, not on a grand or revolutionary scale.

There is a great dualism in society today. It is described, variously, as left *versus* right, conservative *versus* liberal, or traditional *versus* modern. All three descriptions apply in different ways at different times, but the common thread is how all those opposing each other feel excluded. Increasingly, we tend to identify ourselves by these images of exclusion. Everyone seems to feel that they "alone" are alienated. We feel outside of our days. Outside of our work. Finding someone on the left or right who "belongs" is not an easy task. The sense of exclusion has even excluded *belonging*! To me, a great deal of this is rooted in work that doesn't make us feel good, that has too much duty and too little play in it.

The poverty of people even of middle means is disturbing. We hunger for meaning. Our rush to make money, to establish security, to move up, to work two-plus jobs and too rarely have fun, all result in a spiritual poverty. That poverty is all the more ugly because it is so unnecessary. An insatiably greedy economy has targeted the middle class: so many live ensnared by lost equity, unpayable credit card bills, college quandaries, and ever-expanding lists of desires.

We are afraid. We are afraid about our

health insurance. We are afraid about our life insurance. We work several jobs. Everyone is "busy." Busy staving off hunger. Busy dancing to the tune of an economy that has become much too big for its britches, an economy that is a silent partner at the tables in our homes, yelling, "Feed me, feed me."

Fear causes some women to say they "need" their jobs so much they wouldn't think of reporting instances of sexual harassment. Some men report that they don't challenge an unfair boss because they don't want to lose their jobs. If intimidation is not poverty — if, in Shakespeare's words, living "caught in the net they have laid privily for me," is not poverty — I don't know what is.

It doesn't take much to prove the superiority of the play ethic. The play ethic doesn't even have to bring us total peace or happiness to be an improvement over the existing work ethic. The time has come to acknowledge that we are working harder and enjoying it less. The death of the work ethic has already happened spiritually. Bodies still move to its drum beat but hearts and minds don't.

This spiritual poverty is hurting us much more than any alternative possibly could. A man in my former congregation, a Vietnam Vet, aged forty-six, sells and repairs carpet cleaners for a "living." His psychological theme is self-abuse. He speaks of his life as belonging to someone else. He needs to recapture his life but cannot and does not. The odds are stacked against him. A woman and her infant stranded in our local shelter says she'd like to find a horse and ride it out of town. Hers is fantasy escape. They both echo one of Emerson's most famous statements, "Things are in the saddle and ride mankind." Both of these individuals want a house and they want shelter. They have become desperate for these things.

It is this desperation that shows us how work is *not* working. Work does not produce freedom from fear. Rather work seems to lead to more work. Or it leads us to radical dependencies on it.

Each of these individuals, because they were raised in a culture that has taught them that their desperation is their own fault, thinks they should get to a therapist or some other repair person, a fixer — or get a magic horse, or at least a horse that can give a good kick in the butt. It is no accident that addicts say they need their "fix"; they only repeat the typical form of solution, which is outsiders fixing people's insides.

It is the rare individual whose workaday abuse stems from personal fault; more often people have not found their place in their system. They have not understood that the system is not making adequate places for many of us. To create healthy families, we have to get the entire system well.

The first and most practical possibility for each of these individuals is to stop blaming themselves for their lack of place in the system. It is not their fault. Yes, culture conspires to tell them that it is their fault. But it is not.

The practical first step for us is to stop convincing them it is their fault. There are reasons that people are poor or unemployed — and most of the reasons are not laziness, selfishness, stupidity, or any of the other accepted explanations. Most people are poor because others have organized to keep them that way. Maybe not you. Maybe not even me. But by our silence, or our lack of a connecting, we have let the poor be poor. We see a homeless man sleeping on a heat grate and accuse him or pity him, but we don't connect with him. We thank God that we were not a part of the last lay-off. We think it is because we are "better" at working — and the next thing you know, we don't know how to stop working. And in the meantime, we have given the poor nothing but our "spiritualized" care and concern.

What we need is to think deeply, to hear from God and our deepest inners. What is going on in our view of work? How can we come to understand our days? Our time? Who owns it?

As soon as we begin to see ourselves as connected with each other, to think systemically about our cultural family, to see ourselves as parts of wholes, we become capable of understanding matters of the work ethic gone sour. We stop carrying — or dumping — two tons of blame around every day. And that all by itself is Sabbath!

It is astonishing from a political perspective

how little it takes to change a system. Sometimes all that is needed is just a nudge from another direction. "The temptation we must resist," says Bishop John Roach of Minneapolis in *Social Justice: Reviving the Common Good*, "is the one that says that nothing can be done." As the title of Alice Walker's book so marvelously reminds us: *Anything We Love Can Be Saved.*

G. K. Chesterton once observed, "The more modern type of reformer . . . says, 'I don't see the use of this; let us clear it away.' To which the more intelligent type of reformer will do well to answer: 'If you don't see the use of it, I certainly won't let you clear it away. Go and think. Then, when you can come back and tell me that you do see the use of it, I may allow you to destroy it.' "

Once we begin to be able to think and see again, by virtue of the playful any-time time we spend in Sabbath, we realize that even a little will go a long way to change our days. Sabbath seeing, and Sabbath Sense, can change the myth that we *can't* do anything about our days into the reality that we *can*. Anything we say or do has a small effect on the whole and potentially changes it:

"Mr. Jordan, I didn't like the way you handled the problem with Theresa in the office."

"One night a week I will go to the meetings of my local community organization."

Or, as some of the women in the local shelter did, "I will create an economic space for myself by developing a community garden and eating out of it instead of the 7-11."

These actions are little rites of Sabbath, of saying that we belong to our work and our play, that we are not owned. These little actions change things in the system. A father can change a family by small actions: picking up his socks, carrying on conversations where previously he had slept, agreeing to go on family picnics with relatives he doesn't like. A mother can change family by small actions: encouraging others to pick up their own socks, clearly stating her own agenda for a Saturday, ceasing to spend time with people who use her. Ordinary citizens, too, can change their communities on behalf of economic justice.

But it's important to remember that we don't have to change everything or "sacrifice" our life. Rather we have to do definite, concrete, do-able things. Even the smallest of actions will have a wide effect. The worst thing that people can do is work so hard for justice that they develop another reason to insult the Sabbath. That's not Sabbath-Sensible!

Sabbath Sense tells us what is important so that we can make healthy initiatives in our systems. Sabbath Sense yields truth. Economic myopia covers itself in a thin layer of cynicism, all of which believes in the way things are rather than the way Spirit wants things to be. Spirit says, "Mansion, many rooms, lively stones." The world says, "2 BR, no pets, & 750.00 a month, no section 8." There is a

difference in where we should focus our attention —
spiritually, economically, and psychologically.
Without Sabbath Sense, we won't have enough
freedom to imagine Spirit's mansion. With it, we
will.

Sabbath practitioners abound. Marian
Wright Edelman, founder and president of the Children's Defense Fund, puts her eyes on the future and
doesn't allow the status quo to contain her. In *The
Measure of Our Success: A Letter to My Children and
Yours*, she shows what it means to be healthy. She
faces difficulties squarely. She takes direct action.
She does not pretend that things are better than they
are. And she insists that the inner and outer lives of
our nation's children are profoundly connected. She
sees freely. What she sees is justice.

In *Ruby Mae Has Something to Say* by David
Small, the child Ruby Mae gives the spiritual strategy
that connects economic justice with healthy families.
"To achieve universal peace and understanding on
this planet," Small writes, "you have only to speak
plainly, even though you may look foolish. This is a
thousand times better than looking good and talking nonsense." Yes, we may look silly practicing a
play ethic for which no one has given economic or
cultural permission. But remember this: Ruby Mae
wore a large, hatlike "bobatron" (her made-up word
for a silly thing she wore on her head) so she
wouldn't be too shy to say what she wanted! Sometimes being silly is all we need to make Sabbath.

Must we become sour about the economy of the industrial age? Must we reject everything about the old ways in order to practice the new play ethic? I think not. A play ethic disciplines our wanting, not our working, so that that wanting is directed to a purpose larger than the utility of what we are doing. So that we work for Spirit, or justice, or life, or because we want to make the best piece of a car possible on our part of the line. Hooking our labor to a purpose larger than its immediate utility turns work into play.

A better definition of what weekdays need from Sabbath I can't imagine.

chapter five

S*lowing down*

Putting margins on the pages of our days.

Slowing down is an invitation to Sabbath, and Sabbath Sense.

By slowing down every now and then to see what depth and light and wealth we have already been given, right where we are, we can see deeply enough to find grace in the grind.

My advice on slowing down, although simple, is perhaps the hardest step to take: Start your awakened time earlier or your work day later. Think of Sabbath not as rest alone but as the border between rest and work, as a "margin" around the pages of your days. That makes mornings — our daily border between sleep and activity — precious times for Sabbath moments.

Mornings are our page markers, a breath between words, a pause between notes. If we start our day after we have prayed or walked or meditated or journaled, or bowed to the sun, we have already marked the day for which we have awakened.

Many times in my life, I have had to awaken and go straight to duty. I think of the early years of child-raising. Or of the two meetings per month my job requires at our office ninety minutes from home. Or of early, out-bound plane flights. On those days, getting dressed and packed and breakfasted is all I can manage. I hate those days. They go by too fast. They insult time. The entire day, I feel that I am rushing, that I don't have enough time. Time is still there, but I don't see it or acknowledge it. I lose a sense of "enough."

Too many morning rituals are more profane than sacred. They involve a fairly sacrilegious punching of electronic buttons — clock radio, coffee pot, computer. Yet even the mundane has room for Sabbath moments. Most people might think that daily Sabbath should involve deep, quiet, personal prayer. Yet I take a silly pride in acknowledging that listening to the morning news is one of my Sabbath moments. I like to hear twenty minutes of the six a.m. news, the first round, before I get out of bed. I feel robbed if I don't hear the opening segment of "All Things Considered." When Boutros Boutros-Ghali was secretary general of the U.N., l liked knowing what he was doing for the day. I like to hold the world before God. I like to pray for the people whose lives have been invaded by the large or the crazy. My little radio gives me an extraordinary gift. Its signal provides a way for me to have "enough" time because it grounds me in the larger sphere, instead of indulging the fantasy that my life, time, and rounds are overly important. On days that work starts too soon, and I don't have time to listen to the news, I forget to remember. I forget to remember how small I am.

I have another favorite morning Sabbath moment: I love to snuggle and be held in what we call a "sandwich position." When our children were younger, one of them would always come in and sneak between us. They were the "filling." We joked with them and hugged them on their way to their day. This became a family Sabbath ritual because of the time it stole from time for time.

Now that the children are older, they still do it, but less and less. They seem to come into our bed only on the days when something important is happening. They know they can get our attention then. I miss those early mornings of their lives with a kind of ferocity. It is hard to catch them now for a snuggle. They awaken to their own rituals. More often, now, I am the "filling"; they are the quick hug of one piece of bread.

But the fact that they started their days in peaceful hugging for so long gladdens me. The fact that my husband, Warren, and I can still start our days holding each other and listening to the radio also gladdens me. When we lose each other in the day's activities, as surely we must, we can still draw on our deep treasury of morning memories.

I slip out of bed almost regularly at six-twenty a.m. to start the coffee, let out the dog, make sure the sun has risen. In the warmer months, it is my custom to give the cats a good morning on the way out the door, then walk down to the garden. Although this is the most religious-sounding part of my morning, it is really not terribly sacred. It has to do with some impulse to Mecca: I want to orient to the sun, and my garden faces South and East. I also don't want to lose myself too early in the laundry or the breakfast or the packing of files for the car. I fear too hasty an assault on my spirit. So, while the coffee is brewing, I go outside. I bow to the sun.

Unfortunately, most work is now structured to start earlier and earlier and end later and later, if for no other reason than commuting to work is considered normal. For families who have to commute or whose days start earlier and earlier, my advice about lengthening the morning may seem almost cruel. But the same advice must prevail: Start your awakened time earlier or your work day later.

Even when a work day takes ten hours of time, there are still ways to bow to your Mecca. In the car, pray. On coffee breaks, walk. As you wait on "hold" on the telephone, remember Spirit. Choose a daily ritual to mark your Sabbath time, whether it be writing or cooking or reading or praying or meditating. Think of Sabbath-keeping as a matter of spiritual self-defense. In our modern world, we need to steal time from work to play. We must do this. Otherwise work steals us from us.

A street worker in Paris shows the way. On the steps of Sacre Coeur, the great cathedral in the north of Paris, every night young people gather to sing and to dance and to make merry. They sit on the steps of the great cathedral and see the River Seine snake Paris, they see the Eiffel Tower light its jewelry, they see the great shining city spread before them. They have fun. They enjoy a Sabbath, even though many of them may not be old enough to "work." They let time suspend.

Every morning a blue-uniformed Paris street worker arrives at six a.m. to clean up the mess they have made. He confronts debris every dawn. That is his job. The first time I came to watch the dawn at Sacre Coeur, and I saw this poor man face the avalanche of left-over litter, I nearly cried. The second time I watched him pause in his duty and sit down, broom in hand. He took a Sabbath moment on the steps of his work. He made a Sabbath where most of us might not be able. How? He took a break from staring at the garbage and instead gazed at the beautiful city. He made a choice and looked into the dawn. Then he went back to work, refreshed and renewed.

Workers who never rest are awful workers, aren't they? They only *look* like they are working very hard. Their actual productivity is highly questionable. Sabbath does not dethrone work but rather elevates us so that we are more capable for work.

The Zen of having enough time is contained in Sabbath Sense. We work less so we can work better. We work less for the sake of refreshment. We start our awakened time earlier not to have "more" time but rather to structure and deepen the time we do have. We start our work days later to give ourselves to our work with greater zest and give ourselves to our play with greater peace. To experience the time we do have as enough.

That experience — the experience of sufficiency of time and day — is one that comes by marking time into the pieces we want it marked into: time "on" and time "off."

It used to be that the only way I could manage to write was to do so after the kids were awake, and before their breakfast. I would give them an hour of "TV time." My one son always watched ESPN. He was our early bird. The other two children woke up much later, by which time I would have given my day the Sabbath of writing.

I ended this period with a game the children taught me. Each would come into my little writing room, put their hands around my eyes, and ask me to guess who they were. I would always "guess" right via a strategically placed mirror on the bookshelf by my computer. "How do you do that, Mom?" they would always ask. "I guess I just know your smell," I would tease. That particular morning Sabbath ritual marked the borders of my time; it said writing is over and mothering has begun.

I know my own capacity for productivity very well: It is the direct consequence of the time I spend walking, gardening, and writing; the direct result of the time I spend playing ritual games with my children. I know how much I can do if I take Sabbath pauses, and how little I can do if I do not. We all need to pause and refresh ourselves. Once we do, we can slow down. If we do not, we speed up.

The Sabbath-Sense pause can be a catch-up call to your spouse from work. It can be making a grocery list in a meeting where other people think you are taking notes. It can be writing a poem on the back of the accountant's report. Sabbath can be anything it wants to be . . . secret . . . subversive . . . surprising . . . serendipitous. Working but not working. Playing at work. Connecting your inner self to your outer self. Tuning out in order to tune back in. Spontaneous pre-vacationing. Planning a little unplanning.

Unplanned enchantment makes for wonderful Sabbath moments. I cannot praise it enough. Unplanned enchantment can occur when there is just not enough time for everything to go well, when we give up and stop trying to control everything. Unplanned enchantment calls us to interesting delays — delis, friends, donuts, unusual steeples in the clouds. Time to open ourselves up to accidental splendor!

I may have learned this one family excursion when, instead of "enjoying the vacation," my children seemed to prefer stopping at the turnpike bathrooms and playing water games with the pink soap containers and the funny turn-off-yourself faucets. For them, the destination was immaterial, the journey all.

This lesson was underscored by Stripe the caterpillar — found at one of at least thirty-seven pit stops we made while driving through the South. Stripe delighted the children for three-hundred miles, causing them to set aside the strings and strings of Cheerios I had made for their entertainment.

The number of ways my children have tried to educate me about arriving and its disappointments compared to the surprise gifts of journeying is astounding. My son, for example, thinks changing your favorite dessert from pumpkin pie to chocolate pudding is enough excitement for a year. I design trips to the most exquisite pie shop; he prefers the kind, "you know," that comes from the can. Why anything other than macaroni-and-cheese should be served for supper, or anything other than peanut-butter-and-jelly served for lunch, my children don't know.

Why should I tell them? What good will it do for their palate to become as insatiable as mine? Certainly they will be better prepared for the fun of life. Why would I rob them of simple satisfactions in exchange for more sophisticated ones? Ordinary suppers that might bore a jaded adult palate still delight them. Forget following the orders of advertisers urging you reach for all the gusto you can get. No need to respond to ads for the simple life if you must add to your list the procurement of the product that will provide it.

When it comes to Sabbath Sense, children are our teachers.

Unplanning as a strategy cultivates interruptions. It cultivates an awareness of surprise, a capacity to count on the unexpected to get you through the narrow places that tight planning has put you. Unplanning counts on caterpillars showing up on trips.

If you find yourself in a space of unplanned time — stalled in traffic, waiting for someone to show up for a meeting, waiting for a bus or train or plane to arrive — be open to unplanned enchantment rather than using the opening to increase your expectations — and your exasperations.

Even unplanned "disasters" can be mined for Sabbath moments. I remember the twins sitting in their highchairs in our dining room, with its lovely walls painted a soft, dusty rose. I remember them eating borscht, that lovely cold beet soup, which they actually liked. I remember vividly the day they discovered how to *pong* foods with a spoon, and so they *ponged* a simultaneous, direct hit of borscht on the dining room wall. It wouldn't come off, and I considered the dining room permanently scarred.

Yet when we left that house and moved to another city, on my last walk through that empty dining room, I noticed the borscht stains and burst into tears. I considered my grief for my children's fast-disappearing childhood inconsolable. All that time I had hated those stains on the wall, yet eventually they became beloved memories, reminders of how much living went on in that less-than-perfect dining room. If only I could have laughed in the moment . . .

As we open ourselves up to the unplanned enchantment of every-day life, the strangle-hold that work has on our psyches relaxes, and so do we.

As my favorite Jewish deli says, "O.K., just re-lox."

When we slow down, we are choosing the boundaries between work and play. We are declaring that work is not everything to us. That Spirit matters.

chapter six

The unconsumable sabbath

Embracing spiritual leisure.

One of the ways we can tell a Sabbath experience is that we do not pay for it. It does not cost anything. It does not ask us to get out our checkbook or credit card. It is free. But most of us are finding it harder and harder to have a low-cost experience. We pay for our pleasures at a fairly high rate. Sabbath does not imply that paying for things is bad. Rather, it insists that some things are not for sale.

Think of walking. Or dancing. Or singing. Think of dreaming or talking or sitting on the beach. Remember what gardening teaches us. Each of these activities is free enough of outer expense to qualify as a Sabbath.

Walking when you can is Sabbath Sense. Walking gets your pace right in a way that rivals

almost everything else you do. Lunchtime is conven-
ient for some walkers. Mostly I prefer walking in the
late afternoon or evening, the transition time from
being "out" to being "in." I think of the Psalmist's
advice: "In the day, goodness; at night, song." During the day, while I am driving and buzzing about,
I practice goodness, but I cannot "see." While walking, I can refrain from goodness. I can sing. I can see
clearly.

Dancing, especially if it is done in our own
homes or patios or plazas or terraces or clubs or
churches or temples or community centers, provides
the same ability to see. Musician and composer W.
A. Mathieu, author of the *Listening Book*, offers this
tip for turning walking into waltzing:

*"Walking wisdom is natural and lets you learn complex
things easily. While keeping your stride free and even, start
saying left right, left right in time with your legs. Then,
without altering your gait, accent every third word:
LEFT, right, left; RIGHT, left, right; LEFT, right, left;
RIGHT, left, right. You are waltzing and marching
simultaneously."*

I love this idea of dancing as "rhythmic
walking" because it contains the nugget of Sabbath
movement in it. Life that has Sabbath in it has
rhythm. Dancing reminds us of rhythm; walking
slows us down enough to permit rhythm a place in
our days.

Musician Mathieu also tells us, "Walking is a joiner. It merges the inner and the outer world. Go with it. Listen to the teacher inside it. The lesson is useful and free." Mathieu has the Sabbath sensibility down: It joins. It merges inner and outer. We "go" with it. It is a teacher — and the lesson is useful and free.

Walking's rhythm brings with it its own logic. I once had an astounding experience during a walk. I had been thinking deeply about whether women were ever really free. Then these lines from a poem came to mind: "I am a brick in a House/That is being built around your house."

I had not understood the poem in my reading mode. Once I took it out for a walk, it made perfect sense. It took movement to sink its thought into my thought: The time when women are not free is part of the time when we will be free. The past and the present are deeply connected. Houses contain houses which contain houses. The future builds a house around the past.

Many ideas take this level of leisurely rumination. That is Sabbath Sense, freed from consumption for contemplation. We take a break from buying. We "fast" from consumption and nourish ourselves spiritually.

Sabbath gives us time to stop "taking in" and stop "putting out." We let be. We become spiritually healthy.

Spiritual health is getting our human *being*

to lead our human *doing*. The spiritual crisis of our time is that *doing* is leading *being* around by the nose. *Doing* is a false idol: It is supposed to yield security and freedom, but it does not.

Perhaps a caricature of the American dream is embodied in the wish to retire early from human *doing*. Because *doing* has become way too important, we have become ripe for all sorts of false-gods and false-solutions. Our susceptibility to what some criticize as thin, store-bought spirituality — as though more yoga or changed diet would yield the stability of grace to our human *being* — is mightily on the increase. As we suffer more from our daily work and its daily anxieties, we become more needy. Sometimes so needy that we grasp one new pre-fabricated form of spirituality after another, with the same misplaced vigor that we change diets. The consumerist illusion is powerful: We keep shopping for something to balm the soul.

If the only way you can think of to have a Sabbath is to pay for a weekend of it, then by all means have Sabbath that way. But surely there are less expensive alternatives, like a daily walk or a bubble bath on Saturday nights. Or going to church or synagogue or ashram — and resisting pledging until you feel full of Spirit. We do not have to buy Sabbath.

Peace activist William Sloane Coffin constantly tells his listeners that "there are two ways to be rich: One is to have lots of resources; the other is to have few needs." In the playful time of Sabbath, we become aware of how *little* we really do need. That is freedom, especially in our time.

The spiritual urgency of our time does not mean purchasing the right spiritual product. It does not even mean finding out who we are. It is to find out who God is. The spiritual urgency, once graced, is not to get a better job or more money or a more beautiful walk. It is to get more connected to the pleasures of grace. The route is playful, not dutiful.

When I consider the amount of time I have wasted trying to buy the "right" spirituality, I tremble. When I think of the amount of time I have wasted revering the trivial or unimportant — out of sheer confusion more than perfidy — I ache. I have missed more moments of peace and grace than I dare count, so anxious have I been not to miss them.

—— ——

Writing and gardening are two urgent touchstones in my life, things for which I am desperate. Without them, duty reigns. Without them, my *being* has a very hard time finding its way to a crack in my *doing*. But my doing-sensibility is so strong that it can invade even the little time I spend gardening or writing. I have an uncanny ability to turn gardening into duty, writing into deadlines.

Urgency decrees, make the garden absolutely perfect, once and for all. Delphiniums all in this year — no more waiting for the money to buy enough. The garden, of course, has the grace to refuse to oblige. I can weed an entire patch Thursday night and wake up to new weeds Friday morning. I can be sure about the delphiniums in the south corner, so sure that I am broke for a year. But they may not want to breed there. They graciously offer up a failure.

Most of us hate "unfinished." If we start the planting, we want to finish the planting. We hate rough edges. Sometimes frayed edges nearly kill us. We can become captive to our urgency. My urgency about writing is somehow to try to capture the whole thing in one sentence. Fortunately, I fail. In the very urgency to make the thing ordered, in my envy of order, I commit the very lapse that will yield me enough chaos to find Spirit. Garden-variety Sabbath Sense appreciates the paradox and always refuses to end the story early.

My son's teacher taught me about this problem of urgency, of ending the trip along the path of Sabbath too soon. Isaac, who was then seven, came home one day saying that his teacher said stories had to have happy endings. I arrived at the school minutes later, thinking that I would defend God, Spirit, Sabbath, son, and country in commanding that the bad instructions of my parents not inhabit my son. "Don't speak unless you have something good to say," they had told me.

The teacher calmed me down by confusing me. "I didn't say that to all the children, only the children who were getting out of continuing to write their stories by having quick, bad endings," she said. "Every time your son writes a story, he kills the squirrel off in the second paragraph, thus making it unnecessary to go on. I just want him to keep writing and not to trick his way out by stopping the story too soon."

She taught me a respectful fear of deadlines, as though a piece of writing is done just because you hand it in. Or a garden made just because it is planted. Paradox joined her in teaching me to stay on the path eagerly waiting the next curve in the road, the refinishing of the finished moment.

In gardening, this translates to a lengthy permission to let last year's failures compost into next year's brilliance. Best to follow the garden to its seasonal end. Don't "fix" it or buy all the delphiniums at once to finish it.

In our search for God, this translates to being open to uncertainty, to letting grace define us rather than the other way around.

Sabbath is our relief. It is our way out of urgency. It is the turn in the road back to *being*, away from *doing*, back to nonchalance, back to grace. All that is required of us is that we make time to separate duty from grace, purchased from free, labor from rest.

Once we give ourselves the time that Sabbath needs, our urgency dissolves and we manage to care less about the things we love the most. Then we care most about the grace of Spirit, which makes the rest possible.

Why is this age so full of spiritual adventure? We are cursed so severely by duty that we are about to topple over. Our balance is so off that grace must be right around the corner.

We keep thinking that grace is on the other side of the mountain, or on weekends, or after we get a better job. It is not. Or, rather, it is. And it is also right here, right now, but for many of us it is exquisitely hard to locate. The key is Sabbath Sense, keeping Sabbath so that when grace does come along, we are there to receive it.

chapter seven

The summer garden

Creating spirit space.

If Sabbath is to be a part of our lives, we need places and we need meditations. Some people need objects for their meditations, others don't. But we all need some place for Spirit in our home. That makes good Sabbath Sense. Some will balk at the notion of an altar; others will rearrange their entire kitchen or living room around one. Still others will have a simple candle, or one photo, on an uncluttered table. That will be enough for them. There is no one way to fix the spot. The point is, when the Spirit has a place among us, we are able to practice Sabbath there.

Some of the best places for Sabbath to happen is in community, in church, or synagogue, with fellow believers, in a rite that has history to it. The rites and rituals of communal Sabbath — whether mass, or the liturgy, or the Torah — ground us in ancient practice and connect us to an ancient and ongoing people. That grounding may be even more important to contemporary people who feel disconnected, in both inner and outer ways, than it is to those raised in more traditional cultures.

Yet that hour of worship hardly constitutes all of our needs for Sabbath. Beyond the weekly Sabbath of liturgical observance, there are more daily needs for Sabbath: the need for "time off" and "time on," the need for Sabbath Sense in justice, the need of human *being* as respite from human *doing*, the need to embed leisure and perspective deep within us.

For me, building gardens has been a way to create a place in our family for the Spirit in our home. Our kitchen rock garden, for example, provides our breakfast Sabbath.

Let me tell you the story of this garden. We bought a four-acre property in Amherst one November. The old stone walls were crumbling, the browned and deadened perennials only hinted at unidentifiable life. The first spring, our excitement was uncontainable: Everything that came up was a surprise. Lupine! Larkspur! Spearmint!

The second winter we got to work. We decided to develop a rock garden outside the kitchen window. There, though we hadn't been able to see it while everything was growing, was a nice slope and a threshold to the rest of the property. It begged for planting.

We started by gathering rocks from the forest floor. We were lucky in that respect: Many of the rocks were already there, clearly forsaken by previous stone-wall builders. Their odd shapes fit nicely into the slope of the hill.

Rebuilding the stone walls when winter was withholding green proved to be a magnificent job. The cold managed the sweat of the effort. (And balanced my budget! Late winter, if I am not doing something with my garden, I am probably buying something with my credit card. That rock hauling helped with what I call the "unconsumability" of Sabbath.)

Rock gardens may require more labor per square inch than other gardens, but they return with an equal vigor. In the early spring, all I had to do was steal perennials from myself. The white *nicotiana* adored the spot. So did the hollyhocks that climbed the white wall to the kitchen. I moved a couple of roses up near the warmth of the house, and they did better there than the previous winter, forlorn next to the peonies. The real fun was the sunflowers, which planted themselves by the fallen seed from the birdfeeder method. (We are a very self-reliant household and like the ideas of our birds planting their own seed!) An enormous kitchen-window-high bird feeder already stood on the old site, and it became the center piece of the kitchen garden.

Just this year we added what can only be described as a bird hotel. My daughter wrote a murder mystery about the "Hotel Birdslea," the canary that ordered room service, and the paper, *The New Stork Times*, that was delivered to every room, every morning. Her humor has added enormously to the little garden that stays right outside the kitchen window, giving us a place to look for God, when we are wise enough to remember.

The winter joy of this garden is the stone. Summers, it clarifies and matches the flowers, but winters, it displays *itself.* Reginald Farrer, in *The Rock Garden* (1912), says that "stone is never disconnected . . . each block is always, as it were, a word in the sentence."

So it is with our kitchen rock garden. It connects us to the seasons. And because we also hauled rock from the Long Island Sound, where we used to live, it connects us to our old places. Now the children bring rocks back from places we visit for the rock garden. Such is the gift of the Sabbath garden. Always connecting. Keeping things together. As a place for the Spirit in our home, this little area always gives us a lift. It is a physical Sabbath, waiting to be entered.

We also have a garden that the previous owners called "The Chapel Garden" because they made it as an open rectangle, for their children's weddings. It is a large square of lupine and peony. I have added day lilies and daisies and mums — as a way to let my children have ceremonies there in three out of four seasons.

Gardens in all shapes and sizes honor our spiritual desires, our Sabbath Sense. Their quiet pushes a button that switches us to another channel. It is not the channel of the grocery list or the boss' agenda or the children's moods. It is a channel nobody else is on at that moment. Others may think we are thinning the lettuce or picking cucumber. But, aha! We are sneaking a Sabbath moment!

When I get out to the garden, the quiet fertilizes my spirit self. Like most people, I need the cover of useful activity for my praise to erupt. I need the experience of forgiveness that the spinach didn't grow (again!!) to prepare myself for the larger errors in my life. I need a little beauty to burst into song.

I know most people think I'm already being spiritual at my job — after all, I have been a parish pastor more than twenty-five years. My work is just that — work — not terribly different from that of a teacher or a secretary or an editor or a manager.

I do my work at about the same distance from God that most people do their things. If I officiate at a funeral, I am performing more than praying. When I preach a sermon, I am anxious that it flow and communicate. That anxiety, alas, is not worship. I may be even more desperate for the garden than most people; I need the people and their various poverties to go away so I can go toward God.

The garden is a vestment I put on to shelter awareness of Spirit, to shelter prayer. In the garden I am usually on my knees, ready to hear Spirit. Without that kneeling, I get spiritually restless. I can't seem to pray regularly in churches or at any of the appropriate conventional altars, and therefore am dependent on the Temple of the Snow Pea Rows, the Shrine of the Compost, the Holy Water of the Sprinkling Can.

Wasn't it nice, God will say, that you didn't look at your watch or do errands instead of taking your morning garden walk? Making like a human being instead of a clock is such an accomplishment.

Congratulations, God will say, and of course it will be exactly the opposite of what everyone else says. When I am late for the meeting because I stole the errand time from the meeting time, nobody praises me. When the mail and the messages stack up on the kitchen counter like planes over LaGuardia, nobody says congratulations on my pleasant walk. They present their poverties. I present my walk.

Some understand. Most do not. The awareness that Spirit is not greedy in the same way that human beings are greedy is like the magnificence of the lettuce. It approaches the way the cucumbers play hide-and-seek in their dangling glory. These are matters of awe and wonder.

Wonder needs reminders. Without frequent reminders, I am a candidate for guilt trips imposed by meetings and children. I do not choose the oppression of the clock or even the oppression of other people's need of me. I choose lettuce, cucumbers, and peace. That's why I need gardens.

And yet even gardens need Sabbath rest. There is a plant called bittersweet that is legendary on the eastern end of Long Island for the burnt-orange outline it makes of late autumn. It reminds me more of extravagant earrings on a tall, funky woman than of tangled vine. The bittersweet is the garden's farewell song. When its color is gone, winter reigns. The bittersweet portends the long silence of the Spirit we know how to find.

The obvious solution to this winter absence is to learn other channels. Meditation, maybe yoga. Perhaps a lock on the bedroom door and an "accident" happening to the bedroom telephone. Then, again, we could just let winter be and not allow it to become another problem that requires another solution. I could pierce my heart with bittersweet the way others pierce their ears with its likeness. I could let it adorn me, let its signal for the approaching season of rest be part of the wisdom I wear as a person. The bittersweet alerts me that rest is to activity as winter is to summer — in need of each other, somehow even friends. The bittersweet joins all great religions in proclaiming the partnership of opposites. Oddly, I rest in summer while the garden is working. Maybe summer is a Sabbath season for me; winter, a Sabbath season for the garden. When the garden percolates, I rest; when the garden rests, I percolate. May we all experience this perpetual, stone-upon-stone, quiet rhythm of Sabbath Sense.

chapter eight
$\mathcal{T}$*he winter garden*

Creating sabbath respite.

Rocks mean many things to many people. The Irish build altars or cairns in their fields. Christians use rock as imagery for Lord: "The church's one foundation." Helen and Scott Nearing hauled stone for decades to build their "Good Life" house. We all use the slang of being caught between a rock and a hard place.

In China there is an entire science of Geomancy called "Feng Shui" that has to do with the proper location of property with regard to the relationship between wind and water. Ancient peoples have always responded deeply to the natural world in domestic ways. They know about the meaning of wind and water and stone; they make theology out of these meanings. I have often thought that modern suburban life actually squeezes the God out of a place by its flat, homogeneous shapings. Ancient peoples squeezed the Spirit in.

Some say Spirits reside within rocks. Rocks are a way for old altars to meet and become new altars. Perhaps that is why rock gardens are so important to me, why, when I picture creating a place for Sabbath, I think rock gardens are the perfect meditative place. As the great garden writer Gertrude Jekyll put it, "A rock terrace is always congenial to quiet thought."

There is a site on the far end of our property that used to be a genuine sloped rock garden. Because it is far and private, it is there that I want to build the "real" prayer place in our yard, a place for Sabbath respite. This year we just got as far as getting rid of the weeds. The fact that this garden will take many years just to build is a part of its great beauty. It lines itself up with the eternal.

Eternity. Everywhere we go, whether in the great Wall of China, the great castles of Europe, the pyramids of Egypt, or the biblical literature itself, which put the Ten Commandments, supposedly, on real stone, eternity is marked as the rock. Rock is one of the best metaphors we have of everlastingness, and modern people, in particular, need to place rock around them. We need reminders of how long we, and our children, will last.

"Rock," as John Vivian puts it in *Building Stone Walls*, "is as near a definition to forever as exists." He credits gravity with keeping rock sitting on top of itself; I credit larger Spirits, the Spirits within the stones. The foundations of our houses may be slipping, but the rocks are still there, almost begging for the spirit of the householder to reconnect.

But the deeper meaning of a rock garden is in the process of building a quiet corner slowly and meditatively over time. Process over product, journey over destination, a work in progress. It never finishes nor does it have to. It will also last long after you are gone.

At the risk of sounding fanatical, I tell you this: Make your own rock garden. Sabbath will be yours. If you need a devotional spot in your home or garden, rock is a fairly easy and inexpensive way to go. You can make your own seat, or altar, or symbol. If you live in an apartment, you may need to "borrow" a public space for your rock garden, your place of prayer or meditation, your domestic spiritual home. But, even if you have the tiniest bit of property, laying stone is possible for you at home. (You can also lay stones on a dresser and be done with it.)

Determining the spot for a rock garden on your land is easiest in February, before the outline of the land has been changed by greening (and after the snow has cleared, if you live in a northern climate zone). The light of February's elongating days is particularly bright and gives the gardener a welcome chance to evaluate land shapes. The February designer needs to remember that light will be much different in other seasons and not site for winter lighting alone. Another consideration is how the rocks will look in the non-green seasons as well as the green ones. One of the great pleasures of the rock garden is its year-round interest. Thus its shape and its design are as important to the larger eye as the small eye, the distant and the close one.

A south-facing garden is always best if you can do it, but other sites give other obstacles and opportunities. Often the most difficult corner on the property is the best place to use. Rock gardens love nooks and crannies, low spots and high spots.

They like to move themselves to fit the area. Rock gardens are equally open to shade or sun and points in between. And the plants you will eventually choose aren't as fussy as most in terms of soil.

Once you have selected your spot and have an idea of how many stones you will need, or can handle, it is time to begin your search. You may already have seen a crumbled stone wall in a field. Or you may have a rock pile already on the property. Or you may be in need of a back road trip. In New England, particularly, there are thousands of old rock walls dotting the landscape. Many of these have already crumbled.

Gathering fallen stone is not a recommendation to dismantle! Rather it is a slow, almost spiritual, winter activity. Finding and moving stone that has lost its connection to other stone is an act of beautification that can make an extraordinary difference in either a small or large way on a property.

Another meditative way to proceed is to remember which places have been special to you in your life, both near and far. Where do you vacation? Where were you born? Where were you married? It could be time for a return visit to these places to pick up rocks. Small rocks can be as interesting in a rock garden as large ones. While shells often get messy in a garden, sometimes these beach finds have a place in a rock garden. Different types of stones can cohere in silly ways or interesting ways: Keeping them separate enough so that they don't get busy but connecting enough so they show a pattern is the trick. A wave design for a path, for example, can incorporate many varieties.

"Goin' to take a sentimental journey" is not a bad hum for moments like this. (No one has to know you're singing.) And the rock garden that results may or may not want to divulge its sources.

Hauling the stones is the hard part. In the old days people built special equipment to haul the stones they wanted. Today we have to depend on friends. One way to get the rock you want is to have a rock-hauling party. Don't be afraid of large rock! You can get it without killing yourself, but you have to take patience and care. Lift only with your legs. A sprained back may add interest over time to the story of your garden but certainly not in the first few days after the rock arrives!

To move and lift large rock you need a crow bar and a friend. Or a stone boat and a roller so you can ramp the stones to site. Obviously, local stone is the best to use so hauling is kept to a minimum. (On the other hand, I rarely leave a foreign country without one or two rocks in my suitcase. They make excellent souvenirs.)

Once you have your rocks, the goal of arranging them is to keep continuity between them. The best designs happen when every major rock overlaps every other; the worst, when rocks are dots in the middle of dirt. Rocks need to be placed and replaced. Allow for some "give" to avoid frost heaving. Special rocks for corners and turns are the hardest rocks to find. It may take years to find the right rocks.

Shaping or dressing stone can be hard work and is not recommended for the amateur. On the other hand, there are still people expert with the chisel around and, if you have just the right stone, you may want to invest in their expertise. A smoother surface may enhance a wall's appeal.

If you are lucky enough to have water on your property, you may want to consider cairns or piles of rock arranged spiritually and artistically.

Finally you are ready for the joy of planting. Some favorites for rock gardens include the primrose, which is clearly the gem of the rock garden because it requires so little space. The *acaulis* or

English primrose bears a single flower on a short stem; the polyanthus has clusters of flowers on a longer stem. The Garryarde is a short-stemmed polyanthus hybrid from Ireland with unusually dark foliage, while the Juliana is a creeper that thrives in rocky crevices.

The creepers are my idea of survival specialists. They remind me of the poor, as they find and make and keep a place to live. Like the biblical Jacob, they use rock as a pillow and dream great dreams of the holiness of their own crevice.

Echeveria, or hen-and-chick, has several species native to Mexico. They feature involved rosettes of leaves, often with red markings along the tips. They love sun and are succulents, so never overwater; the soil must go dry before watering. They grow very close to the soil line, but as they age they develop a stem. With time, the stem grows taller and taller. The rosette is always clustering at the top. They are very eager to root and will grow quickly. Their value in a rock garden is the way they sneak through crevices to grow, always doing something unusual and unique to their spot. As part of my prayer life, I like having such images to work my own problems through. Sneak through the crevices, I hear Spirit say to me, and grow!

For a more mixed garden, early tulips can be good. They have good carriage. You might also use *Arabis* and Golden Alyssum, *Aubrieta*, *violas*, polyanthus primroses, forget-me-nots, pansies or English daisies. These are all spring-bedding and would need companion planting for other seasons.

Stay clear of big things, like *caladiums*, or Coxcomb or *canna* or *begonia rex*. They overpower the rocks. The same can be true of prayer life. The large is often dangerous to the Spirit.

Finally, good plants can be borrowed from the forest floor. Never take something that is not well-adapted to its own spot. Consider Eurasian wood, columbine, forget-me-nots, *myosotis sylvatica*, Dutchman's breeches, bloodroot, foam flower, any of the *sedums*, and wild blue *phlox*, which makes a sheet of clear blue that is very impressive.

Because rock garden plants are so congenial and grow so quickly if they like their location, they will almost always find their way from a neighbor's yard to yours. If you are only going to live in a place for a short while, and you know it, making horticultural friends is terribly important. They will remember you by what you took from their garden and made grow in yours. They will even tell the next "owner" the story. I have some magnificent red raspberries that still have a now deceased friend's name on them. He gave me two sticks one fall. The patch is now a quarter acre and still marching toward the sun.

What if you go to all this trouble and still don't have the time to Sabbath in the space you have built? Then imagine Sabbath from wherever you are. Recently I mentally reviewed my rock garden while standing in line in the Wichita airport.

Meditation doesn't need real space to be freeing.

Or perhaps you don't have time to linger in your rock garden. A walk there once a day will suffice. Just go to your spot and return from it. The garden will ground you. Sabbath, even a little bit, will still be yours.

chapter nine

Clutter-free living
Making room for sabbath.

Once I spent the night in the ranger's house at the bottom of the Grand Canyon and discovered the best collection of camping equipment and tents and hiking shoes and coolers and backpacks I have ever seen. People, thinking they can climb out of the Grand Canyon, buy hundreds of dollars worth of equipment as their investment in their climbing capacity, and then they discover along the way they just can't carry all that.

So they shed. When they get back up to the rim, other tourists look at them and are amazed the hikers went all the way down, and all the way back up, with just a bottle of water!! Well, they didn't. They littered the trail with their equipment that was too heavy to carry.

One of the main things in the way of Sabbath is clutter. We keep thinking about clearing space, making room, finding time to pick up the clutter we've left along the way. The secret is to stop *thinking* about it and start *doing* it. Instead of acting like Christopher Columbus waiting for the next commission before we can discover the new world, we have to commission ourselves, discipline ourselves, make ourselves declutter. Even fifteen minutes a day, or one corner or one closet per day, will get you to clutter-free living by your next birthday. Or your fiftieth. We do not have to keep preparing, endlessly and compulsively, to unclutter ourselves. We just have to do it.

One of the things lost to the two-career family is cleaning. By the time we get to work, work, shop, and get home, we don't feel that we have the time to keep house. Many people have just abandoned the domestic arts, as though they were unimportant. Homemaking has really suffered — and I'm not sure that office work has improved! Housekeeping and homemaking are crucial to the ability to separate "on" time from "off " time. A sense of place is crucial to the ability to rest.

In our family, the day begins only when the clutter of yesterday has been cleared to make space for today. We make at least a minimal clearing of the decks. With a family of five — a number that often temporarily multiplies — this sometimes means an astounding amount of picking up. On days when there is not enough time to declutter the whole place, we simply pick up everything that is out of place and dump it in a big laundry basket.

Decluttering in our family also means empowering and deputizing the children — who is going to do what, when. I love it when they say at breakfast, "Mom, how is it going to be for me today?" They mean the laying out of the plan. "Empowering" means clearing the confusion off the table, making choices about what can and cannot happen.

The same is true for decluttering unfinished emotional business. There may be sneakers on the floor in more ways than one. Someone may have been hurt and not yet let it go. Picking up the emotional pieces may mean remembering, or writing down, the more delicate or emotional matters for later talk. "Empowering" for the coming day involves looking back, as well as looking forward, and making sure there is enough space for forgiveness.

As important as daily decluttering rituals are, seasonal cleaning is important for a good clearing. Any house that is good enough to live in is good enough to spring clean. Our homes deserve the decluttering and the polishing and shining of a caretaker who annually or semi-annually loves it back to new-ish.

Every once in a while, even if we practice sneaking a little more Sabbath into work or airport lines or gardening, we have to prepare beautiful, lengthy, extravagant Sabbaths. We have to prepare our homes for Sabbath, as observant Jewish women have done for centuries. We have to prepare a special place. To arrange the setting. To locate the right dishes. To bake a bread. To clear the space.

I'm not talking about hiring one of those vans ("Mighty Maid" or whoever) to pull up in the driveway with underpaid workers, major heavy-duty equipment, and zoom cleaning. Sure, when you come home at the end of the day, things look clean. All the Legos and Mighty Morphin Power-Ranger helmets and Ninja Turtle masks missing for months are sitting on the dining room table, mute testimony to the honesty of Mighty Maid — and the impersonality of their cleaning job. If you had done the spring cleaning yourself, all these precious homeless objects would have been rediscovered joy-fully, given shelter. The children would have a kind of secure gladness: Once their precious plastics were lost, now they are found.

The virtues of doing our own spring cleaning are unsung. Most of our houses are wearing the layered look. Last week's dominos sit under the previous week's art museum souvenirs, under which are the guides to Paris from the untaken trip. The newspapers have been recycled, but the birthday party invitations went with them. That beautiful pitcher from New Mexico would be beautiful if you could see if from behind its camouflage.

When we do our own spring cleaning, we get down to basics. We declutter and de-layer. We throw the things out that are threatening to permanently cloud our vision. The lovely things we do have get the space they need: They get new frames, new perches, new points of view on the rest of us. Possessions, I believe, need a Sabbath as much as people.

Spring cleaning has only one big negative: It takes time. Time that otherwise could be spent worrying about what a mess our house (and life) is. Clutter and dirt are spiritual metaphors — never deny it. The art of decluttering and cleaning are epically biblical in proportion. They precede Sabbath as Thursday comes before Friday.

What does Spirit require of us? "To restore streets to dwell in." I wonder what God's point of view is on hallways and stairways and closets and what remains of the alley between the bed and the dresser. Probably not quite as serious. Restoring is a big project; spring cleaning is small one. Yet in each activity, we are employing Sabbath Sense. We are finding ways to have enough time. We are taking back the time that has been stolen from us and squandered on worry.

On the other hand, there is no need to overdo cleaning. Even a Saturday afternoon in which we say we are spring cleaning could elicit the ritual nature and virtue of the matter. If we are too far cluttered to clean the whole house in a given day or season, then we could settle for a corner. A finely prepared corner. And then just sit there for the weekend, turning our backs on the rest of the mess.

Too often, chaos has come to reign in our homes and calendars. Our homes are nests where our life adds up . . . to a negative number. Our clutter builds, accumulates, and threatens to obliterate us. For many of us, the rooms we use are indeed fatally busy. The rooms we don't use are dangerously unused. They are for storage, as though we have stored the soul's opportunities for waiting and aloneness, as though Sabbath were an old luxury, wasted on our modern "with-it" sensibility.

Spring comes and goes with no Sabbath cleaning. Fall arrives with the same lack of announcement. Children spend days looking for things that might have been important to them if they could have found them.

The problem isn't the chaos of modern houses so much as it is the sense of *defeated* chaos. Spring cleaning doesn't abolish chaos but rather liberates it from defeat, something like the French poet's concept in "Le Bateau Ivre": "Peninsulas washed adrift from their moorings never experienced a more triumphant chaos." Spring cleaning lets drifting moorings live a more triumphant chaos. That is the only goal it dares. Sabbath is not compulsive order; it is creative order. As such, it can include all the chaos it needs to include. Still, it triumphs, chaos and all.

I think houses are more like bodies than anything else: They are one of our skins, one of our layers. I imagine an Old-House Heaven for unloved houses, estranged from their householders. Mornings, these houses cry for what happened to homemaking as an occupation. Afternoons, these houses cry in remembrance of their busy interiors. Every now and then, though, a house comes along that has been loved into luster and luminosity. Loved beyond clean, into triumphant chaos. *Glad-mess!* A house that was touched every now and then with a rag saved and softened for that purpose. When that house comes into Old-House Heaven, it gets the evenings. It tells stories of how much fun it was to be alive. It gives advice on polishes. It tidies up the cushions for the support groups the next day before it goes to bed. Sometimes it spring cleans Heaven, just for fun. Just to make sure the flowers are fresh at least once a season.

In that house, Sabbath is queen.

One summer I discovered my mother-in-law frantically cleaning out her dresser drawers. When I asked her what she was doing, she said she had discovered a lump in her breast. "I want to make sure, if I die, that things are in order."

More than one of us feels threatened by the lack of order in our lives. For many of us, travel is more free than home if for no other reason than that we are carrying only a bag or two instead of a lot of rooms. More than one of us feels that if we could just keep our houses from overwhelming us, maybe we could be well.

One form of wellness is living on the other side of clutter, in a place called clarity. Such clarity is truly a spiritual, not a physical, place. I try to live a few inches ahead of the layers of my life, as a "high-nester." This is one of the elements of Sabbath: living *above* our mess, not *in* our mess.

I understand completely what my mother-in-law was doing that day: She was trying to move beyond clutter. Decluttering is a break in the build-up of matter. It is a time to reflect on matter from a point of view beyond matter. It is definitely a spiritual matter.

We can find the clutter-free life spiritually or physically. We can find it at home or while on the road. I spend a lot of time in religious retreat centers, and I spend a fair amount of time in motels as well. One is simple, sparse, uncluttered. The other is cold, neat, impersonal. One has all I need; the other has more than I need. One has Ivory soap; the other, little bottles of lotions and shampoo. One is cheap; the other, expensive. One is low stress on the environment; the other, high stress. In the one, I leave often full enough of heart to want to give an additional contribution. In the other, I always feel like I overpaid at the end.

I go from one way of life to the other. I know which one I like the best. The uncluttered life is the one for me. Ready in an instant — burdens shed, traveling light — for the wondrous vistas of the Grand Canyon. Capable of Sabbath at a moment's notice.

chapter ten

S*piritual fitness*

Allowing for the unfinished.

Sabbath Sense invites us to look for spiritual nourishment in unusual places. If we are mindfully attentive to each moment, we can bring Sabbath into the events of our lives, for any occasion, no matter how humble.

In even the simplest thing there is a banquet for the Spirit. Consider the Zen "raisin meditation." Slowly, reflectively chew the same raisin as long as you can, *one lowly raisin*, without swallowing it, paying mind to what you taste, feel, sense, think. Gradually, that simple, homely, shriveled, wizened former grape can become an astonishing symphony of flavors, textures, surfaces, and reveries, verging on an epiphany — an illumination — just as a tea-cake crumb triggered the lush memories of

Proust's masterpiece, *Remembrance of Things Past*. Sabbath moments can be cultivated in even the most minute details.

One of the great things about Sabbath's unlocking the key to our time is an opportunity to fully experience the things that happen to us. Many of us have too many undigested experiences wandering around inside us. Sabbath Sense lets us know our own narrative. We see what has happened to us. We become acquainted with the shades and shapes, the tastes and textures of our stories. We take time to think, to ruminate on the "raisin."

Making time for Sabbath means taking time to listen inwardly while looking at the outward commonplace. I like to use this litany of invitation for listening:

> Listen deeply.
> Stay still until you hear
>   what you are listening for.
> Insist on the ancient wisdom
>   that body and soul are linked.
> Listen for how they link now.

Our musings may not lead us to comfortable places. Sabbath time may take us to places where we see ourselves and who we are, lumps and all. Sabbath can be "serious" rest, a time of mining sometimes painful experiences for their deeper meaning. Surely there is time and space for forgiveness. We don't need to be so afraid of getting it right, right away. We do have time. We have Sabbath time.

Inner spiritual fitness will have to come by negotiating the rough inner waters. If we can wade through that turbulent spiritual water, we can begin to find the grace from which to tell our story — even if it is a only story about the wading.

Ancient peoples affirmed only spirit. Moderns affirmed only matter. Both failed to comprehend God. The spiritually fit person will tell a story about their experience that affirms both matter and spirit, ancient and modern, doing and being. The spiritually fit person:

- ⬥ includes rather than excludes
- ⬥ knits back together the separateness of work and play
- ⬥ reunites *doing* and *being*
- ⬥ has a spirit place
- ⬥ never eats without thanking somebody
- ⬥ declutters spiritually
- ⬥ grows something
- ⬥ refuses to let all time be the same

Sabbath Sense is the strategy for any spiritual fitness plan. As is already terribly obvious, my personal Sabbath strategies are my garden and my writing. I evangelize about each of these frequently because they give me a simple enough story about which to effervesce. Formal religion has not done that for me for a long time. If it does again, I'm sure I will let someone know. I do not find God so much in religion but rather outside and under religion. In religion I am a *doer*; outside I have the space for *being*. Churches, too often, are infatuated with excessive activity; they/we work ourselves to death. In Sabbath Sense, we have a chance to play, to *be*. Church still gives me glimpses of God but only when it puts a fence around its self-promotion and opens the door to expose God's interests. I am embarrassed at this but not surprised. Even the work of clergy has been invaded by culture's work ethic.

When we take back our time, and go inward, we will be able to again turn outward and face the larger issues that are splitting people apart. If present trends continue, and centralized institutions of worship crumble, I fear we will have failed to feed the spiritual and religious hunger of the public, failed to provide shelter for the spiritually homeless. We will have rearranged the chairs while the people starved.

Inner Sabbath can restore spiritual health to our religious institutions at a grass-roots level. Neither New Age spirituality alone nor old-time religion can solve the spiritual dilemma of modern people. That is very clear.

In my sermons and stories, I say God's action lets this century's religious failures become next century's hopes. I want to learn from mistakes.

From problems. From difficulty. From failure. In the church, conflict can expose the way forward. In gardening, that translates into using compost to grow new plants. In writing, that translates into using our very mistakes, our grief, to improve our writing. "Nothing bad ever happens to a writer," says an old story that loves paradox as much as I.

Our failures are precisely the spiritual task of the moment. We must get very well acquainted with them. Get on a first name basis with them. We must articulate them, learn them, love them, repent them, revise and remake them. That, too, is part of Sabbath Sense.

We may not find our wholeness as a people until well into the next century. But we will find it. As Elizabeth Barrett Browning said, "All that I had Hoped to Be and Was not/Comforts Me." In taking the time for Sabbath, we as a people — even we as a church — can be healed, restored, put back together again.

Spiritual fitness is surely at least this possibility. And not just in the garden or the solitude of the study. Also in the world. In our institutions. Among the poor. Among the dailiness of our efforts, and even our failures. Spiritual fitness increases the possibility of spiritual flexibility, that grand understanding that we dare move. That "Here" is not final. Nor is "There."

There is no question that our best chance at spiritual fitness, Sabbath Sense, has been stolen from us — and we think of ourselves as the freest people in the world! What we need to do is to use our freedom to stem this theft of our own time.

Let the women show the way. As I see it, women are less rigid than men right now. More flexible. Perhaps because we have been broken apart at the level of body and soul and worked to heal ourselves. Perhaps because we are making peace between our interiority and our institutions, between our personal Sabbaths of housecleaning and rock garden-making and the cultural Sabbaths of Sundays and Saturdays.

I am reminded of Aristophanes' drama *Lysistrata*, that ancient Greek play in which women withheld sex so their men would stop making war. "*Lysistrata* was an attempt to stem the rush toward annihilation, to save something from the wreckage before it was too late to save anything," writes translator Dudley Fitts, "an attempt to make laughter succeed where rage and tears . . . had failed."

In its purest form, Sabbath Sense calls us to laughter to save us from the wreckage of human overdoing. Spiritual fitness calls us to connect with time beyond time, with space beyond space. Calls us to connect with the moment precisely because it is connected to the other moments. To connect with ourselves precisely because we are connected to each other. Spiritual fitness remembers that we live, now, in eternity.

chapter eleven

S*abbath rituals*

Taking back our time.

To a child, birthdays, anniversaries, Christmas, and Hanukkah are all sacred. They lift time above the ordinary. They lift things like daily suppers above the routine. Cake may be a child's communion! I once watched five children who didn't really know each other share a box of Munchkins in a train car. That experience was "eucharistic" for them. The holiday of the train was being celebrated.

Holidays give us time to celebrate and enjoy each other. In our family on our children's birthdays, we often give a special gift to someone in need, as a way to thank God for our own child. Recently we were lucky enough to be invited to buy a brick in a new walkway leading to a fountain in our town. The children are very proud of their names written in stone.

In Decembers, we give a gift equal to the size of our current family Christmas budget to Heifer International, a group that sends animals to farmers around the world to foster self-reliance. It is our ritual to pick which animals we will give. One very expensive Christmas we were able to send a water buffalo to the Philippines! Special foods, special gifts — "specialing" our children and just one or two more of the world's children — are important to us. It deepens our Holiday joy. And it makes Sabbath Sense.

Religious institutions also help us keep Sabbath. The obvious ways are in weekly religious observance. The less obvious way is through a yearly calendar. Jews have one; Christians have one; Moslems have one. Each of these calendars mark the year.

These calendars have much in common: In the dark season, we prepare ourselves for the light. There is a penitential period, a time for fasting. Then comes a time to celebrate the glorious victory of life over death, good over evil.

When we mark our spiritual time in these ways, we separate one kind of time from another, which is the brilliance, the sense, of Sabbath-keeping. We expect different kinds of time. We anticipate huge dollops of meaning to be added to our lives. *Kairos*, special time, joins *chronos*, regular time. It is a Sabbath-Sense habit to honor time.

One Ash Wednesday, we had a brilliant ice storm in Western Massachusetts. Every inch of everything outside was covered. I had to chip a block of ice off my car at six a.m. and then drive up into the Berkshires for a meeting. There was a permeation of ice that was dazzling.

That afternoon, at the end of the morning's penitence, the sun came out and the ice melted. I imagined this as the grandness of God's grace. The way it washes away our errors. The way it warms us. The way it forgives us. The way it changes us.

And I recalled how one of the *t'ai chi* postures is about ice becoming water, becoming gas, in the process of healing. The stage toward water is when the sages imagine sickness digging in, unless it melts quickly.

There was a lot of damage in this ice storm. But as great as the damage, even greater was the healing. As strong as the ice, even stronger was the sun. I count on such a melting down to happen as often as possible in my life. Until the heart melts and it finds the words, we won't know forgiveness. An ice storm may find a way of speaking deeply through us and our days.

Mercy, Madeleine L'Engle reminds us in the title of her book, is *A Live Coal in the Sea*. The sea is God; the sin is the coal. When we get that proportion right, we can find mercy. Sabbath seasons and rituals always get the spiritual proportions right: They show us what is truly large in life.

The "proper" way to keep Sabbath is not the point: The point is the perspective of our hearts. It is what athletes call being in "the zone," what I have called here the right separations of time. There is a season for everything, and "a time," as Ecclesiastes puts it, "for every purpose under heaven."

Yesterday I drove to one of our churches with an old friend. We came to a dirt road that was full of spring mud and ruts. A farmer came out of his house and said, "Do you really want to go down that road?" We said yes, it was our favorite back way deep into the woods.

We proceeded down the rutted road as far as we could go — and we had to turn around! There was no way we were going to make it through. We ended up having to back out the whole way.

We both had quite the laugh — and something to muse on for a long time. Yes, to everything there is a season! At least now we know how to recognize mud season when we see it.

Sabbath-keeping helps us remember the seasonality of life and promises that the seasons will keep changing. In the Jewish faith, there is a special season called Jubilee that takes Sabbath Sense to a whole new level, giving it exciting economic/political/ecological implications.

The provisions for Jubilee are that every seventh year debts are canceled, the oppressed set free, the land is allowed to lie fallow. "The Jubilee vision weaves together economic and ecological justice, work and rest, liturgy and society. Jubilee invites [us] to live in holy rhythms — a beckoning invitation to . . . release, liberation," writes Will O'Brien in *The Other Side* magazine. During the fiftieth year — after seven times seven years, or forty-nine years — there is a special Sabbath of the Jubilee. Jubilee presents a powerful vision of a Sabbatical for the planet!

In her wonderful book *Jubilee Time: Celebrating Women, Spirit, and the Advent of Age,* Maria Harris uses the ancient Hebrew season as a way for women to joyously come to terms with middle age. Think of looking forward to our Jubilee Years instead of lamenting the loss of our looks! Jubilee moves from the mundane trap of chronological time into the blessed reality of kairotic or special time.

Jubilee belongs in our lives right now.

But for Jubilee to arrive, we first must be able to imagine it. We must make space for it. Open our hearts. Declutter our homes. Clean off our slates. Take down our fences and redraw our boundaries. Mulch our gardens. Prepare a plain new page. Only then can we leap the fence of daily time into more universal time. Then we will reconnect the isolated days and years into holy time.

One of my favorite pastors said, "To move fast on this corner requires standing still most of the time." Sabbath is a time of standing and being still, long enough, that we see into the depth of time.

"You bring me news of a door that opens at the end of a corridor, sunlight and singing, when I had felt sure that every corridor only led to another, or to a blank wall," wrote T. S. Eliot. Substitute the word "Sabbath" for the "you" in this sentence, and this is a picture of a Jubilee that could set us all free. Jubilee is the Sabbath of Sabbaths, the Summary of Sabbath Sense.

One forty-year-old man I know has described his life as "having missed every train I should have caught." There is no doubt that he lives a deep disappointment. He lives a longing for a past he did not have. Most of us sense that we missed some train we should have caught. But we can be saved by imagining a different future. A Jubilee time.

There is an aspect of imagining Jubilee that has to do with endurance. Since we can't immediately implement complete personal or societal make-overs, we need to start with the small things that can be adjusted in our lives. Like being less perfectionistic. Like offering prayer at meals, or songs at night, or observing a weekly communal Sabbath, or building a rock garden to remember God. Like making friends with a person of a different race or age or occupation. Like breaking our enslavement to our clocks and calendars. (What God has put together as universal time we have put asunder as calendar time.) Like believing in a deeper sense of time, and river, and rock.

Sometimes the best we can do is to last long enough for a new Jubilee time to come. To wait, for the next cycle of possibility. Or belief.

Remember the great Old Testament story of Jacob. He had to use a rock as a pillow. There Jehovah let him rest and visited him. Jacob waited for Jubilee.

Shall we work for the time of Jubilee? I think not. Let us rather wait, expectantly, and rest, for it. Let us muse on it during our Sabbaths, whether they be in a rock garden, while walking, or worshipping.

There's a beautiful spot near where I live in New England at the Westfield River where people have built a marvelous brookside series of cairns, beautiful rock piles that make a monument to what I don't know, evoking a congregation watching a waterfall. A rock garden built by no one anyone knows, used by the public, as delightful a spot for meditation as I know.

Like the Westfield River's breathtaking rock sculptures, we could wait, and watch, and worship. Soon, then, if we are patient, the Sabbath of Sabbaths will surely come.

The simple stones cry out for Sabbath. So do our imaginations. Let them be strong, like the stone, awaiting an artistic reassembly in connected time. When Sabbath and eternity make sense, here and now.

———   ———

DONNA SCHAPER is an Area Minister (Regional Officer) in the United Church of Christ. Formerly a parish pastor for over twenty-five years, she now has episcopal responsibility for over one hundred churches in the Western Area of Massachusetts. After her graduation from the University of Chicago Divinity School and ordination in 1973 (as one of the first women to be ordained), she served as Urban Minister at Tabernacle Church in Philadelphia. During that time, she co-founded Women Organized Against Rape (WOAR), one of the first such organizations in the country. From Philadelphia, Schaper went to New Haven, where she served as Associate Chaplain at Yale University. She trained Yale students in community organization and established a Community Economic Development Project that was among the first nationwide to experiment with using church endowments as capital for community projects.

Schaper's other commitments and accomplishments have included serving as Executive Director of Urban Academy in Chicago and as the weekend commentator for Channel 12 NEWS, Long Island. She has written for such diverse publications as *The Catholic Reporter, Organic Gardening, Greenprints, Christian Century, The Christian Science Monitor, The New York Times, Upper Room, Unity, The Other Side,* and *Christianity and Crisis.* Her most recent books include *Why Write Letters?, Calmly Plotting the Resurrection, Hope in Hard Times, Shelter for the Spiritually Homeless,* and *Teaching My Daughter to Mulch.*

Currently, Donna Schaper lives with her husband, Warren Goldstein, and their three children on a small organic farm in South Amherst, Massachusetts.

CPSIA information can be obtained
at www.ICGtesting.com
Printed in the USA
FFOW02n1621220115
10504FF